Open Education and Education for Openness

EDUCATIONAL FUTURES
RETHINKING THEORY AND PRACTICE
Volume 27

Scope
This series maps the emergent field of educational futures. It will commission books on the futures of education in relation to the question of globalisation and knowledge economy. It seeks authors who can demonstrate their understanding of discourses of the knowledge and learning economies. It aspires to build a consistent approach to educational futures in terms of traditional methods, including scenario planning and foresight, as well as imaginative narratives, and it will examine examples of futures research in education, pedagogical experiments, new utopian thinking, and educational policy futures with a strong accent on actual policies and examples.

OPEN EDUCATION AND EDUCATION FOR OPENNESS

Edited by

Michael A. Peters
University of Illinois at Urbana-Champaign, USA

Rodrigo G. Britez
University of Illinois at Urbana-Champaign, USA

SENSE PUBLISHERS
ROTTERDAM / TAIPEI

A C.I.P. record for this book is available from the Library of Congress.

ISBN 978-90-8790-679-5 (paperback)
ISBN 978-90-8790-680-1 (hardback)
ISBN 978-90-8790-681-8 (e-book)

Published by: Sense Publishers,
P.O. Box 21858, 3001 AW
Rotterdam, The Netherlands
http://www.sensepublishers.com

Printed on acid-free paper

TABLE OF CONTENTS

FOREWORD

As the Dean of the College at the University of Illinois at Urbana-Champaign I am delighted to be able to write a foreword to this edited collection of essays on 'open education.' As the editors, Michael A Peters and Rodrigo Britez explain so well in their Introduction, 'open education' is a project that embodies a political, economic, social and economic set of broader goals and aspirations. In one obvious sense the *project* of open education dates back to Enlightenment values concerning universal access to knowledge, to information and to education—values that found expression in the early prototypes and the Declaration of the Rights of Man formulated in the late eighteenth century. These particular political values and the wider set of which there are a part—values fundamentally connected to the Enlightenment narrative and struggle for freedom—received a new expression through advanced technologies in information and communication in the late twentieth century, especially through the development of the Internet. These technologies helped to design and engineer large-scale peer-to-peer architectures that encourage an ethic of mass participation and co-creation. The advent of the PC, the economics of computing and file-sharing, and the mass production of microprocessors, eventually brought down the cost of copies, distribution and dissemination providing the ideal conditions for the much touted knowledge economy and what we can think of today as the '*open* knowledge economy.' This new paradigm of social and cultural production is a mode of the organization of knowledge that provides for the rapid spread of public knowledges and free knowledge flows across all kinds of traditional boundaries and borders, not least that set which is bound up with the development of the modern nation-state and its emphasis on a bounded territoriality and a fierce economic nationalism.

Today the promise of open education is genuinely emancipatory in grand old sense of the Enlightenment narrative based as it is on a commitment to greater and (eventually) universal access to knowledge, information and education. This is the point of 'education for openness' that promotes both a greater self-awareness and reflexivity about the nature and promise of open education considered as a global project, perhaps even as a commitment to the means of developing global citizenship.

The claims for open education as a new social movement remain to be seen. This collection of essays is one of the first books to examine its origins and application. The book itself, as the editors, explain emerged out of a Masters class taught by Professor Michael A. Peters and assisted by Rodrigo Britez in 2008 ("Open Source, Open Access, Open Education") as an elective in the Global Studies Program at the College of Education. The essays are the product of assignments by students who were encouraged from the outset to consider the possibility of a publication as part of the class with the goal of investigating, popularizing, and evaluating 'open education'. This collection is therefore also designed to demonstrate a new spirit of student, peer and student-professor collaborations that are very much a part of 'open education'. I am more than happy to recommend this collection as an early exploratory and experimental collection that embodies the spirit of collaboration that springs from the practice and promise of 'open education'.

Mary Kalantziz
Dean of Education
University of Illinois at Urbana-Champaign,
6th September, 2008

PREFACE

The essays in this collection were written for a class taught by Michael Peters. The class itself was located within a graduate program in Global Studies in Education (GSE) at the University of Illinois at Urbana-Champaign. GSE has two components: an on-line Masters program that enables teachers from around the world to have a rich and productive dialogue, beyond borders, about teaching in a world that is increasingly interconnected (see gse.ed.uiuc.edu), and an on-campus doctoral program designed to help students develop new knowledge about the complex processes of globalization and the ways in which these are reshaping educational policy and practice. Innovation and creativity lie at the heart of GSE, not only in our theorizing about global issues and futures but also in the manner in which we practice pedagogic relations. We use new technologies to broaden the scope of our learning. We try to examine old issues in education in new and fresh ways, and seek to understand the changing conditions of globalization and the educational realities to which they have given rise.

We all know how neo-liberal globalization has produced unequal and uneven social and educational consequences, and how global integration of economy, facilitated by the new developments in information and communication, has occurred in a space characterized by asymmetrical relations of power. While the notion of global connectivity has been hailed for its potential to liberate human relations from the confinement of artificial national boundaries, it is equally clear that it has disrupted, even destroyed, the lives of many people and communities. In education, while many have been able to take advantage of global interconnectivity and mobility, others have been left behind, trapped within the cycles of poverty and unequal opportunities. Despite their cosmopolitan promise, new media technologies, so often noted as the key driver of globalization, have reproduced patterns of cultural and linguistic privileges, now at a global level.

It is within this broader context of these contrasting interpretations of globalization that GSE is located. Our pedagogic challenge is not only to understand patterns of social and educational inequality but also to imagine how a different globalization might be possible – how globalized education might become an instrument of ethical possibilities that not only stresses access to literacy and technology but also considers how democratic, civil and human rights could be extended, how environmentally-friendly production systems could be promoted, how women and other historically disadvantaged groups could be empowered, and how greater intercultural understanding could be realized through greater access to information and the formation of learning communities across the globe.

The course taught by Michel Peters demanded from students an understanding of the role information and communication technologies play in global reconfigurations. More specifically it required them to think about the potential of the Open Source movement for opening up new communication systems, for promoting effective cross-cultural dialogue and for realizing the democratizing possibilities of education. The three key terms of the course –open source, open access and open education —were constantly problematized with respect to the ways in which they might be related. In this sense, the discussion worked at each of descriptive, analytical, normative and imaginative levels simultaneously. It brought together on-campus and on-line students into a productive dialogue, challenging them to work beyond the binary between physical and virtual spaces. It encouraged students to explore some of the more complex issues surrounding new technologies and new media, and how we might interpret the notions of open source and open access in world of digital divide. But equally it explored their potential for the development of open education and open society. The notion of open itself became a key point of debate.

Each of the papers in this collection wrestles with these issues, hoping to illuminate the economic, political and cultural complexities surrounding the Open Source movement. Rather than simply repeating the celebratory rhetoric of its highly passionate advocates, these papers struggle with the challenges it poses for thinking seriously about knowledge creation, management and dissemination. I have no doubt that these papers will generate an intense and productive dialogue. No one interested in the potential of new media for realizing democratic goals —the goals of open education – can ask for any more!

Fazal Rizvi
Director, Program in Global Studies in Education,
University of Illinois at Urbana-Champaign

ACKNOWLEDGEMENTS

This collection of essays is the result of a project that has changed in multiple ways over time. The beginning of this book's idea can be found in the online Program for Global Studies in Education (GSE) at the University of Illinois. GSE offered a space for the development of a course to study the plethora of online open education resources, which is now available for teachers and universities. Those resources are an important innovation that promise future changes for higher education.

By reflecting on the nature of open education resources, the question on openness for education emerges. What is remarkable today are the ways that teachers and institutions now begin to form part of the processes of global exchange and production of a 'pool' of global educational commons. The question about the significance of this development, their limits and the consequences for practitioners and institutions from the perspective of teachers is extremely complex. For example, the policy agenda of institutions, states, and international organizations related to the regulation of new technologies facilitates the existence and viability of those resources. This has consequences to the ways that those resources are used and produced by educators.

At the same time, the new paradigms of production and collaboration, pedagogy and communication of open content questions the nature, limits, and promises of openness in education through new technologies. Promises and expectations for the spread of freedom and social justice are at the core of our belief on education. The prospect of at least partially fulfilling these promises through the emergence of the open education movement is at the heart of the dialogues with teachers and students whose questions are the genesis of this collection.

We wish to acknowledge and thank Fazal Rizvi and the members, the faculty, and the students of GSE for providing us with the opportunity to bring this project forward. We also like to thank Ergin Bulut for his assistance in formatting various chapters of this book. However responsibility for any errors within the text lies with the Editors.

Finally, we would like to thank Lea Goode-Harris for graciously allowing us to use her work 'Poetree Labyrinth' created for the Labyrinth Guild of New England Festival 2005 as the cover of this book. Her painting can be found online at www.srlabyrinthfoundation.com.

The tree in the painting goes with a poem that makes us think about one of the purposes of this book; to explore today's potential promises and meanings that openness offers for education.

Be joyful together,
Oh, Beloved Comforter
embrace magnificence magical Mystery,
Joy is returning from Shadow into Light

reflecting awe filled community,
Jangly, jangly, I pirouette into openness...
The creaky floor emanates warmth...
To fully expand brings light and peace...
Allowing openness, finding Blessings and coming home...
We choose to walk where we remember that we are all one...
Awakening to community and care...
I dance the shining lightness of being...
The engineers are not disturbed by the non-linearity,
Imagine the joy of the Holy now...
Open my heart, Encourage my soul,
Each step, music illuminating my soul...
A clear day and no memories!
No one is ever alone on the path to fulfillment[1]

NOTES

[1] This poem by Jeanne Colbath, Frank Sandstrom, Tricia Kibbe, Bevan C. Tulk, Beth Mace, Lucy Crichton, Mathew Gallelli, Deborah Jackson, Peter Vernam, David Strohmeyer, Karen Hope Montgomery, Nancy Ballantyne, Helen Curry, Pura Gomez, Barb Ducharme, Hallie Sawyers, Sunny Davidson, Suzan Scott Strohmeyer, Ann Boedecker, Adam Kibbe, and Mia Corinha can be found online at the website of the labyrinth foundation: www.srlabyrinthfoundation.com [blog: http://lealabyrinth.typepad.com]

NOTES ON CONTRIBUTORS

Daniel Araya is a doctoral student in Educational Policy at the University of Illinois (Urbana-Champaign). The focus of his research is the convergent impact of network technologies and cultural globalization on learning and education. Daniel has published on various subjects including peer-to-peer networks, the knowledge economy, democratic innovation, open design, cultural hybridity, and the cosmo-politanization of the University. He is currently working as a graduate assistant with the Global Studies in Education graduate program and the Cyber-education program at the National Center for Supercomputing Applications (NCSA).

Rodrigo G. Britez is a doctoral student in Educational Policy at the University of Illinois (Urbana-Champaign). He was born in Argentina, grew up in Paraguay and came to the United States as a Fulbright scholar. His major research interests include: globalisation and education policy, higher education policy in South America, and networks of governance in higher education policy. He is currently working on issues relating to social networks and the role of trans-national agencies in policy processes in higher education.

Heidi A. Knobloch is a Special Education teacher at Cunningham Children's Home in Urbana, IL where she has worked for the past three years teaching secondary students with behavior disorders. She received her B.S. in Special Education from University of Illinois Champaign-Urbana. She recently graduated from the University of Illinois Champaign-Urbana with her Ed. M in Global Educational Policy. Her specific interests in Global Educational Policy include volatile nation-states in Africa, philosophical implications on policy, and social justice through education.

Faith McKinney was born and raised in Tokyo, Japan. Coming to America in 1979, was a reverse culture shock that had a great impact on her life. She attended Concordia University in Austin, Texas and graduated with my Bachelor of Arts in Education and Music. After teaching elementary through high school for quite a few years and working with various companies, she and her husband moved to Irvine, California in the fall of 2003 to work at Concordia University, Irvine, California. The first two years she was the Shenzhen Program Coordinator, working with teachers from Shenzhen, China who came to the university to study. In January 2006, she started working as the Master's in Arts in International Studies Program Coordinator. It was a new program so she helped to develop and enhance the program to make it a more enriching overseas experience for our students. In May of 2008 she received her Masters of Education in Educational Policy Studies. She also began a new job at California State University in Fullerton as Program Developer for the International Programs Asia.

Williams Montepeque is a Spanish teacher in Emmaus High School in Emmaus PA, where he has worked the past three years. He received his B.S. degree in Education with a concentration in Spanish, from Kutztown University of PA. He recently received his Ed.M. degree in Educational Policy and Globalization from the University of Illinois Urbana-Champaign. His interests are to pursue an Ed.M. in Educational Technology to better serve his students in using technology in the classroom.

Lucinda Morgan is the Language Development Coordinator at the Grand Canadian Academy in Nanjing, China, where she has worked the past three years. Prior to this, she worked for three years for a Chinese NGO teaching at teacher training colleges in Shandong and Jiangsu Provinces. She received her B.A. degree in East Asian Studies, minor in Religion, from Wittenberg University and is currently pursuing her Ed.M. in Educational Policy and Globalization from the University of Illinois Urbana-Champaign.

Michael A. Peters is Professor of Education at the University of Illinois at Urbana Champaign (US) and Adjunct Professor in the School of Art, Royal Melbourne Institute of Technology, Australia. He won a first in Philosophy and completed a PhD in the philosophy of education, focusing on Ludwing Wittgenstein, at the University of Auckland (NZ) where he was appointed to a personal chair in 20000 and held a joint position between Auckland and Glasgow. He writes at the intersection of fields in philosophy, education, policy and politics, with a strong interest in theories of post-modernity, knowledge and economy, and implications for education. He has written over 50 books and some 300 articles and chapters, including most recently *Showing and doing: Wittgenstein as pedagogical philosopher* (2007, Paradigm) (with Nick Burbules and Paul Smeyers), *Truth and subjectivity: Foucault, education and the culture of self* (2007, Peter Lang), *Building knowledge cultures: Educational and development in the age of knowledge capitalism* (2006, Rowman & Littlefield), (all with Tina (A.C.) Besley), and *Knowledge economy, development and the future of the university* (2007, Sense). Michael A Peters is professor of education at the University of Illinois at Urbana-Champaign and adjunct professor at the School of Art the Royal Melbourne Institute of Technology.

Linda Smith Tabb is the Coordinator of Online Programs in the Department of Educational Policy Studies in the College of Education at the University of Illinois at Urbana-Champaign. She has been on the faculty of Parkland College in Champaign, Illinois for ten years, where she has taught courses in French, Spanish and humanities. She received her B.A. with distinction in French from the University of Virginia, her M.A. in French Linguistics, and Ed.M. in Educational Policy Studies from the University of Illinois at Urbana-Champaign, and is currently pursuing her PhD. in Educational Policy Studies from the University of Illinois at Urbana-Champaign. Her interests include globalization and education, open source and open access in the teaching and learning of foreign languages, second language acquisition, language policy, and the cultural premises of study abroad.

Shivali Tukdeo is a doctoral candidate in the department of Educational Policy Studies, University of Illinois at Urbana Champaign and she has been working with Global Studies in Education program for over four years. Her doctoral research focuses on the connections between social networks, transnational advocacy groups and educational policy production. Other areas of her research interests include Language Teaching, Teacher Education and International Education.

Gabriela Walker is a doctoral student at the University of Illinois at Urbana-Champaign (UIUC) in the Educational Policy Studies department. Mrs. Walker obtained her B.A. and M.S. degrees in psychology and special education and, respectively, inclusive education at the University of Bucharest, Romania, and continued to study special education at the University of Georgia, U.S.A, where she earned her Education Specialist degree. Her research interests are global educational policies with an emphasis on European and special educational policies, and applied teaching methodologies with students with special needs, especially students with Intellectual Disabilities and Autism Spectrum Disorders. Gabriela's work experiences include news-related editorial work at various newspapers in Romania, teaching children with a range of special education needs both in Romania and the U.S., and teaching undergraduate and graduate level courses in the U.S.

MICHAEL A. PETERS & RODRIGO G. BRITEZ

INTRODUCTION

Open Education and Education for Openness

Open education involves a commitment to openness and is therefore inevitably a political and social project. The concept of openness in regard to education predates the openness movement that begins with free software and open source in the mid 1980s with roots going back to the Enlightenment that are bound up with the philosophical foundations of modern education with its commitments to freedom, citizenship, knowledge for all, social progress and individual transformation. Chapter 1 explains these early origins and also the basis for open education in a variety of forms from the 'open classroom' to the 'open university'. Yet in another way political, social and technological developments have taken place in parallel alongside the history of the movement of open education that have heightened certain political and epistemological features and technological enabled others that emphasize questions of access to knowledge, the co-production and co-design of educational programs and of knowledge, the sharing, use, reuse and modification of resources while enhancing the ethics of participation and collaboration. Open education as a movement sits within the broader framework of the history of openness that brings together a number of disciplines and fields to impact directly upon the value of knowledge and learning, their geographic distribution and ownership, and their organization.

Openness is a concept that has come to characterize knowledge and communication systems, epistemologies, society and politics, institutions or organizations, and individual personalities. In essence, openness in all these dimensions refers to a kind of *transparency* which is the opposite of secrecy and most often this transparency is seen in terms of access to information especially within organization, institutions or societies. Certainly, this is part of the meaning of openness in relation to politics and societies—openness implies a form of open government which demands that citizens have access to official information and that reasonable grounds are advanced for withholding information from the public domain. This is the basis for the movement of freedom of information that led to the passage of legislation concerned with rights to information beginning with the Freedom of Information Act passed in the U.S. in 1966 and by seventy countries around the world since then. Freedom of information means that the public has enforceable rights to access records and information held by government or public bodies. Such freedom of information is seen to be integral to democracy considered as a form of open government where government decision-making at all levels is transparent, public records are open to public scrutiny, and individuals have rights of access to such information. The doctrine of open government is related to the theory of free inquiry and the free expression of opinion based on traditional freedoms such as freedom of speech, freedom to publish, and freedom of the press. It originates in Enlightenment philosophies that are the basis for modern theories of rights and stands against state secrecy and the use of state secrecy against its citizens.

In terms of organization and institutions, openness has come to mean a certain mode of operation characterized by cooperative or collaborative management motivated by the belief that democracy provides a set of principles not only for civil society but also for public and private organizations. Often this mode of organizational openness is associated with features of democratic procedure including open meetings, free debate, elected positions, and voting as a means of decision-making. Most often open meeting procedures are followed. Such organizations and institutions make use of flat hierarchies and consensus decision-making.

The political and organizational levels are given direct application, philosophical speaking, in the concept of the 'open society' which the French philosopher Henri Bergson first used to identify those dynamic societies no longer tied to a static kind of tribalism and the Viennese philosopher Karl Popper developed in the Cold War context as a concept for defending liberal politics against communism and state totalitarianism (closed societies). Karl Popper's notion of the open society also, at least implicitly, is associated with his epistemological doctrine of critical rationalism or 'falsificationism' that holds that science progresses through criticism and that claims to knowledge should be open to empirical testing and falsification. In a clear sense, then, openness can also be construed as an epistemological doctrine that also implies a central role for science and philosophy as one of the central means for achieving a rational society based on its openness to criticism. Stated in this general way Popper's doctrine is consonant with principles of criticism that begin the modern project dating from Kant's *Critique of Pure Reason* or Descartes' *Discourse on Method* insofar as criticism is the source of rationality and modernity both in its literary-historical as well as its scientific-technological senses.

This sort of account in its general form also allows for counter-Enlightenment strand of thinking such as Romanticism that wants to criticize and question the very commitments of modernity by pointing to the pitfalls of rationalism and forms of rationalization in modern society that have compromised freedom and led to excessive regimentation and bureaucratization of society. The ecological critique of industrialism might also be seen to belong to this counter-Enlightenment form of criticism as might some forms of postmodernism.

Open education in terms of its most recent developments cannot be separated from the development of open systems and the history of open source, open access, open archiving, and open publishing. Education has always been dependent to some degree on changing information and communication technologies from the abacus and stone tablet to the blackboard and computer. The more critical questions is to understand how these new technologies, and especially Web 2.0 platforms and protocols, promote a ubiquitous learning that collapses spaces between school and home, work and school, work and personal interest, teacher and student and so on, transforming formal education and the market and creating new forms of social production that are essential to the knowledge economy.

Openness also has a line of thinking that directly ties it to individuals and their psychological make-up. Openness is one of the five personality traits empirically established in research dating from the 1930s that has come to serve as a model of personality (along with conscientiousness, extraversion, agreeableness, and neuroticism). Openness is sometimes interpreted as 'intellect', seen as 'openness to experience' and associated with appreciation of art, curiosity, adventure and the imagination. Open people who are regarded as experimental, creative, curious, less thrown by complexity and subtlety, are contrasted with closed people who may be more conservative, less flexible, more bound by habit, resistant to change, and tied to the security of a familiar environment. We might even talk loosely here of open personalities as 'global' personalities. Openness in this context has a great deal to do with education for it has been argued since days of Rousseau and 'philosophers of free play' for children (Pestalozzi, Froebel, Montessori and even Dewey) that openness to experience is an educational important value and that unstructured play (freedom) is one of the best ways of encouraging curiosity and experiment.

It is clear that there is a vital historical and political framework that embraces a variety of perspectives of freedom and openness that are part of the commitments of open education—commitments that lie deeply woven into the fabric of modern education as it developed during the Enlightenment and thereafter. Part of the project of *education for openness* is to identify and to recognize these deep commitments and to provide a theoretical context for viewing and understanding claims to openness and freedom in education within this context. Education for openness is about a meta-awareness of the political, social, economic and technological frameworks that enable and permit greater world democratic use and reuse of educational resources and programs through new technologies enhancing the virtues of openness such as the ethics of participation, collaboration and co-production, co-design and co-evaluation of all aspects of education. In this way education for openness is also about exploring the possibilities of open education in both its historical and future perspectives, and the encouragement of greater dialogue across all boundaries. In this sense the project has a world-historical component that is visionary in its commitment to principles of open inquiry, open access, open collaboration and leadership, and to education role in promoting open democracy at a grass-roots level, that is, through the everyday actions of students and teachers who communicate and exchange ideas and resources across time and space.

Open education and education for openness are related projects and perhaps one of the most significant educational movements to surface in the twenty-first century.

About this book

This book originated as part of an online-only course delivered in the Department of Educational Policy Studies at University of Illinois at Urbana-Champaign by Michael A Peters with the graduate assistance of Rodrigo Britez. The course entitled *Open Source, Open Access, Open Education* was developed by Peters and Britez as part of the new Masters Global Studies in Education Program. The course was developed in 2007 and taught for the first time in 2008. The course description reads as follows:

> The present decade can be called the 'open' decade (open source, open systems, open standards, open archives, open everything) just as the 1990s were called the 'electronic' decade (e-text, e-learning, e-commerce, e-governance). This course will introduce course participants to the emergent paradigm of Open Education (OE): first, by setting the scene briefly outlining the challenges of higher education represented by globalization, the knowledge economy and the development of e-learning; second, by reviewing and concept and contemporary forms of 'openness', including open source, open access and the 'open society'; third, by providing a grounding in the state of the field of open education, including related topics like copyright, licensing and sustainability; and, fourth, by encouraging you to think and act creatively about current practices and possible alternative practices in open education.

The course sessions had the common purpose of inviting the reflexion and exploration on the current meanings of open education and openness for educators, learners and higher education institutions. It included the study of major reports about Open Education, lectures and discussions exploring 'openness' and the meaning of open society, and explored the more important open education projects. Furthermore, it included discussions on open access, open source, copyright and the public domain and the ways in which educators are licensing open education resources.

Each session was organized as an exercise to answer and ask questions about some of the crucial challenges that the growing provision of open education alternatives through new informational technologies seem to promise for education. Examples of recurrent questions were: what is open education and why this idea should be pursued through open access to free, high-quality educational opportunity? In which ways is it pursued today by education institutions and how this is related not only to informational technologies but to new economic paradigms of organization and production? What are the purposes of open education and how will the future of higher education look like as result of this development?

All these questions and many more that emerged from the discussions and rich debates attempted to offer a glimpse on Open Education and Openness, their consequences, practice and limits, which are echoed through the chapters of this book.

The Organization of this Book

This volume is organized in three parts. The first part is concerned with the ways in which new technologies create new possibilities and boundaries for the participation in and access to education. The chapters in this part are concerned with complex questions about the implicit paradigm of openness and collaboration in education that these developments promise. In considering these issues, this part illustrates the way in which a more 'democratic' system of knowledge production and distribution still operates through an overlapping and diverse assembly of institutional and technological boundaries that are defining the limits and potential future of Open Education projects.

As Daniel Araya points in chapter 2, one of the fundamentals of new systems of innovation anchored in new technologies is their potential for advancing systems of education. However, the implications of open education for institutions of education, as Michael Peters indicates, are still related with contested ideas about the meaning, of the ethics of openness and freedom that predate the emergence of informational technologies.

The final two chapters of the first part by Rodrigo Britez and Shivali Tukdeo, provide nuanced accounts on the ways that the promises of openness in education are related with practical and ethical questions about political freedom, access and the role of states and global institutions in the regulation of technological infrastructures. These chapters indicate that the power and reach of new forms of participation, collaboration and innovation in education through new informational technologies is contingent on the development of specific policy environments for society at large attuned with values of transparency, participation, intellectual and political freedom for the production and access to knowledge not limited to education institutions nor subservient on the needs of a 'global knowledge economy'.

The implications of open education are producing distinct impacts at the local, national, regional and global level, and they vary according to the different policy and socio-economical contexts in which they are implemented. The four chapters in this part explore the development of open source and open access initiatives in Latin America, Africa, Rumania and China. These chapters show the challenges and uneven institutional, political, economical and technological terrain in which open education initiatives are taking place. Heidi A. Knobloch describes Africa's biggest problems of poverty, debt, food insecurities, and lack of clean water not only as negatively affecting the development of individuals but also as hindering future development by nations by impeding the free flow of educational opportunities. Will Montepeque explores the Open Source movement and the challenges and opportunities that the provision and access to educational resources through digital technologies creates for Latin American countries. An interesting question that this chapter evokes on the shared difficulties with countries in the African context is: How can developing countries provide more technology in the classroom or society if they cannot provide communities with textbooks and supplies for schools? As Gabriela Walker's chapter on Romania's open source and education initiatives indicates, Information and Communication Technology (ICT) has the potential for a powerful impact on the development of educational opportunities in the twenty first century. The chapter describes the global nature, of pressures and challenges impelling the emergence of open education initiatives through the prism of the global digital connect and disconnect and Romania's contribution to the development of open source. The final chapter of this part, by Lucinda Morgan, is concerned with the role of the Chinese government in fostering open education and open source initiatives at the same time that it pursues the construction of censorship systems for information, hindering the access to internet resources. The article provides nuances on the important role that the Chinese state policies play in fostering or hindering open source, open access, and online education initiatives. Among those, issues of language, quality and absence of regulated standards for the provision of online education offer a complex picture of the current state of those initiatives.

In final part of the book, Linda Smith Tabb and Faith McKinney explore the pedagogical practices implicit in the open education paradigm and the use of new informational technologies. Faith McKinney reviews the way in which open education initiatives are creating an array of open educational resources for teachers. At the same time, the chapter indicates the new challenges for educators in teaching using the open content of K-12 learning resources available online in the United States today. Among those, there are problems of access to basic infrastructure in schools, and technological gaps for different groups of teachers and students. The chapter indicates that lack of training, access to technological support and equipment are still noticeable for particular demographic and geographic groups. In these instances the author asks the following important question about the reach of open education resources in a context in which enormous disparities are observed in advanced industrial countries like the U.S.: 'how can we expect them to be accessed from other countries that have less technology access than the United States?'

In the final chapter, Tabb explores the ways in which language learning supported by open content and tools online could provide interesting possibilities in the field of second language acquisition. The chapter shows some of the most recent research and theories highlight some advantages of the open education ecosystem, at a time when there is a disconnect between policy and best practices in the United States, in the area of foreign language education.

This books ends with a challenge for those engaged in exploring the potential impacts and possibilities of open education initiatives. The open education paradigm and its consequences for educators and learners speak of an uneven geography where the access to technological infrastructure does not necessarily imply freedom or openness. In those instances, openness in education related to open education initiatives requires an engagement in research about the ways in which policy, cultural, digital and educational environments facilitate a political commitment to open systems of knowledge production and distribution.

Michael A. Peters
Department of Educational Policy Studies,
University of Illinois at Urbana-Champaign

Rodrigo G. Britez
Department of Educational Policies Studies,
University of Illinois at Urbana- Champaign

THEORETICAL AND PHILOSOPHICAL CONSIDERATIONS

MICHAEL A. PETERS

1. THE HISTORY AND EMERGENT PARADIGM OF OPEN EDUCATION

We cannot teach another person directly; we can only facilitate his learning.
Carl Rogers, 1969

The operation of a peer-matching network would be simple. The user would identify himself by name and address and describe the activity for which he sought a peer. A computer would send him back the names and addresses of all those who had inserted the same description. It is amazing that such a simple utility has never been used on a broad scale for publicly valued activity. —Ivan Illich, 1971

INTRODUCTION

On February 14 2008 Harvard University's Faculty of Arts and Sciences adopted a policy that requires faculty members to allow the university to make their scholarly articles available free online. The new policy makes Harvard the first university in the United States to mandate open access to its faculty members' research publications (Suber[1]) and marks the beginning of a new era that will encourage other U.S. universities to do the same. Open access, to use Suber's definition, means 'putting peer-reviewed scientific and scholarly literature on the internet, making it available free of charge and free of most copyright and licensing restrictions, and removing the barriers to serious research.' As Lila Guterman reports in *The Chronicle of Higher Education News Blog* 'Stuart M. Shieber, a professor of computer science at Harvard who proposed the new policy, said after the vote in a news release that the decision "should be a very powerful message to the academic community that we want and should have more control over how our work is used and disseminated."'[2]

Open access has transformed the world of scholarship and since the early 2000s with major OA statements starting with Budapest in 2002 movement has picked up momentum and developed a clear political ethos. Harvard's adoption of the new policy follows hard on the heels of open access mandates passed within months of each other – the National Institutes of Health (NIH) and the European Research Council (ERC). As one blogger remarked: 'open archiving of peer-reviewed journal literature [is] now on an irreversible course of expansion'[3] not only as U.S. universities follow Harvard's lead but also as open archiving makes available learning material to anyone including students and faculty from developing and

M.A. Peters and R.G. Britez (eds.), Open Education and Education for Openness, 3–15.

transition countries. Harvard's adoption of the open archiving mandate is similar in scope to the step taken by MIT to adopt OpenCourseWare (OCW) in 2001. These initiatives are part of *emerging knowledge ecologies* that will determine the future of scholarly publishing challenging commercial publishing business models and raising broader and deeper questions about content development processes as well as questions of resourcing and sustainability.

The Ithaca Report, *University Publishing In A Digital Age* (2007) indicates that there have been huge changes in creation, production and consumption of scholarly resources with the 'creation of new formats made possible by digital technologies, ultimately allowing scholars to work in deeply integrated electronic research and publishing environments that will enable real-time dissemination, collaboration, dynamically-updated content, and usage of new media' (p. 4). As the report goes on to mention alongside these changes in content creation and publication 'alternative distribution models (institutional repositories, pre-print servers, open access journals) have also arisen with the aim to broaden access, reduce costs, and enable open sharing of content' (p. 4).[4]

We can consider open publishing, open access and archiving as parts of the wider movement called *Open Education* that builds on the nested and evolving convergences of open source, open access and open science, and also emblematic of a set of still wider political and economic changes that ushers in 'social production' as an aspect of the global digital economy, an economy that is both fragile and volatile as the current world credit and banking crisis demonstrates so well. The present decade can be called the 'open' decade (open source, open systems, open standards, open archives, open everything) just as the 1990s were called the 'electronic' decade (e-text, e-learning, e-commerce, e-governance) (Materu, 2004). And yet it is more than just a 'decade' that follows the electronic innovations of the 1990s; it is a change of philosophy and ethos, a set of inter-related and complex changes that transforms markets and the mode of production, ushering in a new collection of values based on openness, the ethic of participation and peer-to-peer collaboration. In a fundamental sense it also represents the continuation of a meta-story, albeit in a new register, of freedom. In the postscript to *Building Knowledge Cultures: Education and Development in the Age of Knowledge Capitalism* (Peters & Besley, 2006) we made the argument that

> there has been a shift from an underlying metaphysics of production—a 'productionist' metaphysics—to a metaphysics of consumption and we must now come to understand the new logics and different patterns of cultural consumption in the areas of new media where symbolic analysis becomes a habitual and daily activity. Here the interlocking sets of enhanced mobility of capital, services, and ideas, and the new logics of consumption become all important. These new communicational practices and cross-border flows cannot be effectively policed. More provocatively we might argue, the global informational commons is an emerging infrastructure for the emergence of a civil society still yet unborn.

We also emphasized the link of this new logic of consumption to a classical concept of freedom:

> Information is the vital element in a 'new' politics and economy that links space, knowledge and capital in networked practices. Freedom is an essential ingredient in this equation if these network practices develop or transform themselves into knowledge cultures. The specific politics and eco-cybernetic rationalities that accompany an informational global capitalism comprised of new multinational edutainment agglomerations are clearly capable of colonizing the emergent ecology of info-social networks and preventing the development of knowledge cultures based on non-proprietary modes of knowledge production and exchange.

Since writing these words my research has focused increasingly on issues to do with the production and consumption of knowledge within the digital knowledge economy and a special focus on the notion of 'openness' considered in epistemological, ethical and political terms. At the University of Illinois (Urbana Champaign) I have been involved in a number of courses, journal issues and publications that explore the dimensions of 'open knowledge production systems,' a term I first used in 2007 in an introduction to a symposium in the journal *Policy Futures in Education*[5] to discuss John Willenski's (2006) excellent book *The Access Principle: The Case For Open Access To Research And Scholarship.*[6] As Editor of the journal *Policy Futures in Education,* I published Cushla Kapitzke's special issue on the ethics of copyright and patents with John Willinski and Richard Stallman (Director of the Free Software Foundation) as contributors among others. This issue was later published in revised form as *Global Knowledge Cultures* (Kapitkze and Peters, 2007) together with an essay I wrote on 'informational democracy'.

Policy Futures published a special issue on *Digital Libraries* with Ruth Rikowski & Isaac Hunter Dunlap as guest editors (vol. 6 no 1) and a symposium on Yochai Benkler's (2006) *The Wealth of Nations: How Social Production Transforms Markets and Freedom* with contributions from Philippe Aigrain, Leslie Chan, Jean-Claude Guédon, John Willinsky, and with a response by Yochai Benkler (vol 6, no 2). In a forthcoming issue (2008, vol 6, no 4) entitled *Commercialisation, Internationalisation and the Internet* Chris Armbruster explores a range of issues related to commercialization.

I built upon the work of *Building Knowledge Cultures* with a book entitled *Knowledge Economy, Development and the Future of the University* (Peters, 2007a) that reflects on the role of the modern university in a global networked economy.[7] I gave a keynote address at the Spanish Research Council's sponsored Conference on the Book (Common Ground Publishing) at the invitation of my colleague Professor Bill Cope, held in Madrid late 2007 'Opening the Book' (Peters, 2007b). In this paper I discuss one aspect of messianic line of thinking about e-texts that I have called simply 'openness' going back to Walter Benjamin and entertain the concept of 'open knowledge production systems' that in my view will not mean the 'end of the book' but its radical subsumption in a new electronic

5

textual system involving a set of changes in all aspects of the 'culture of the book' including all phases of its creation, production and consumption as well as its practices and institutions of reading and writing.

In terms of courses I have held a number of Advanced Seminars at the University of Illinois at Urbana-Champaign, including: 'Knowledge Futures in Higher Education: Knowledge, Freedom and Development' which included a linkup to World University Network's (WUN) *Horizons Virtual Seminar Series: Global Knowledge Futures* (2005)[8]; 'Education and Development in Higher Education' (with Fazal Rizvi) (2006); 'Knowledge Systems, Scientific Communication & Academic Publishing in Higher Education' (with Bill Cope) (2007); as well as a number of online-only classes at the Masters level using Moodle and Elluminate, including 'School-based project in Internationalization' (2007); 'Open Source, Open Access, Open Education'[9] (2008); and 'Global Citizenship Education' (2009). I mention these classes because for me there is a very strong link between teaching and research and working with graduate students. I use these class sessions to theorize much of the work that later appears in published work. The experience and practice of e-learning, online teaching and e-publishing work is a necessary part of the ability to theorize.

This chapter builds on those experiences and embodies a variant of the same story continuing the same line of argument by providing a history of 'open education' and theorizing the emergent paradigm of Open Education (OE). The term 'open educational resources' first came into use at a conference hosted by UNESCO in 2002 where it was defined as 'the open provision of educational resources, enabled by information and communication technologies, for consultation, use and adaptation by a community of users for noncommercial purposes.' As the OECD report (2007: pp. 30–31) notes:

The definition of OER now most often used is: "open educational resources are digitised materials offered freely and openly for educators, students and self-learners to use and reuse for teaching, learning and research". To clarify further, OER is said to include:
– Learning content: Full courses, courseware, content modules, learning objects, collections and journals.
– Tools: Software to support the development, use, reuse and delivery of learning content, including searching and organisation of content, content and learning management systems, content development tools, and online learning communities.
– Implementation resources: Intellectual property licences to promote open publishing of materials, design principles of best practice and localise content. (OECD, 2007: pp. 30–31)

In the first section this chapter provides a very brief history of 'openness' in education by linking it to a successive series of utopian historical moments based on a set of similar ideas stemming from core Enlightenment concepts of freedom, equality, democracy and creativity. In the second section it plots the dimensions of the emerging paradigm of Open Education by reviewing four major reports that have been released during the last year or two.

THE UTOPIAN HISTORY OF 'OPENNESS' IN EDUCATION: FROM THE OPEN CLASSROOM TO OCW

We can group the appearance of the notion 'openness' in education around a successive series of utopian historical moments based on a set of similar ideas stemming from core Enlightenment concepts of freedom, equality, democracy and creativity. The early history of open education consists political and psychological experiments conducted in special schools established in the early twentieth century. The movement from the very beginning thus was shaped by contemporary political and psychological theory that attempted to provide alternatives to the mainstream that was connected to and exemplified a form of society and set of institutions that was seen as politically desirable. These early ideas that also significantly involved an analysis of the space and architecture of schools and the associated idea of freedom of movement underwent considerable refinement and development over the course of the twentieth century. An important aspect concerned not only the analysis of architecture but also the overcoming of distance in a form of distance education that began in the late nineteenth century through correspondence and progressed through various media eras including that of radio and television. 'Open education' consisted of several strands and movements that often coalesced and overlapped to create a complex skein that despite the complexity was able to rapidly avail itself of new communication and information technologies in the last decade of the twentieth century and to identify itself more broadly with the new convergences among open source, open access, and open courseware movements. It was as though the open education movement in its infancy required the technological infrastructure to emerge as a major new paradigm rather than a set of small-scale and experimental alternatives or a form of distance education. We can chart these utopian moments in terms of five historical moments:
- The Open Classroom;
- Open Schooling;
- The Open University;
- Open Courseware;
- Open Education.

The movement for openness in education was anticipated by a range of models after those of Homer Lane and A.S. Neill and, to a lesser degree, Bertrand Russell's libertarian school, all established in the early twentieth century. All three thinkers were wedded to the classical enlightenment doctrine of freedom and autonomy in education even though they tended to give it expression through then contemporary psychological theory influenced by Freud concerning child rearing. Lane established Little Commonwealth at Evershot, Dorset in 1913. Influenced by the group therapy movement he emphasized 'shared responsibility' and freedom of 'self-expression.' A.S. Neill, a follower of both Lane and Wilhelm Reich, the controversial psychoanalyst, established Summerhill in 1921 on the basis of a concept of personal freedom and equality that he held were important for learning and the development of self. Ideas of freedom and democracy also figured in Carl Rogers' (1969) *Freedom to Learn* written under the influence of the therapeutic movement including Otto Rank and existentialist philosophers like Martin Buber and Søren Kierkegaard.

Rogers emphasized 'self-directed learning' and facilitation rather than teaching as he entertained strong doubts about the necessary connection between teaching and learning. In the same environment Everett Reimer's and Ivan Illich's influential works during the 1970s, most famously in *Deschooling Society* (Illich, 1972), argued formal education had confused schooling and education and created a kind of psychological impotency that delivered a stultified and non-creative uniformity.

In a broad sense these ideas were also given a concrete expression in the 'open classroom' movement which originated in Leicestershire and was based on freedom of movement, the importance of 'play' and a novel analysis of the space and architecture of schools. In Britain the movement became known as 'informal education' based on 'learning by doing' in home-like settings or 'learning centers' where pupils were encouraged to be self-directed and creative in 'schools without walls'. The *Plowden Report* (1966) in the UK outlined a philosophy of primary schooling based firmed on Piagetian stage theory that emphasized children as individuals and supported a move to child-centered methods and curricula suited to the 'needs of the child.' Open schooling as 'informal education'–informed by both Romantic thinkers like Rousseau, Pestalozzi, and Froebel and later, of course, Dewey–emphasized process over structure, dialogue rather than formal instruction, democracy rather than control, freedom and self-expression over teacher-directedness and authority. A number of texts of the time explored the relation between open education, freedom and knowledge (Nyberg, 1975), the relation between the open school and the open society (Puckrose, 1975), or emphasized the link with 'community' and the move away from hierarchy (Easthope, 1975).

Informal education tended to emphasize alternatives based on opening up traditional processes and structures of the school and decoupling the school from specific location or internal architecture, an age-cohort, or dependent upon a single source of authority. The unschooling, homeschooling and community-schooling movements, for instance, focused on self-direction (autodidacticism) and harnessing community institutions and resources found in museums, local libraries and even mass media. The informal education movement also had strong links with 'adult education' and, later, the concept of lifelong learning.

Distance education began in the late nineteenth century and was initially based on correspondence a tradition based on early international science that survived in 'correspondence schools' where children were isolated in rural areas and separated from local schools by great distances. Instructional radio was introduced much later though its utopian promise was never fulfilled. Similar when instructional television began transmitting courses in the early 1930s. The model of technology-based distance education really received its impetus in the 1960s when the Open University in the UK was established founded on the idea that communications technology could extend advanced degree learning to those people who for a variety of reasons could not easily attend campus universities. It is interesting that the Open University really began with the BBC and ideas for a 'wireless university' or 'teleuniversity' that could combine broadcast lectures with correspondence texts and visits to local universities. From the start the idea of the 'open university' was conceived as a response to the problem of exclusion. The Open University (http://www.open.ac.uk/

advertises itself as based on 'open learning' which is explained in terms of 'learning in your own time by reading course material, working on course activities, writing assignments and perhaps working with other students.' The Open University has around 150,000 undergraduate and more than 30,000 postgraduate students. 10,000 of our students have disabilities. It has been immensely influential as a model for other countries and distance education flourished in the 1970s and picked up new open education dimensions with the introduction of local area network environments.[10]

Open courseware (OCW) is very much a feature of the twenty-first century. MIT, one of the first universities to introduce OCW, announced its intention in the *New York Times* in 2001, formed the OpenCourseWare Consortium in 2005, and by 2007 published virtually all its courses online. This is how the MIT website expresses the history of OCW

> MIT OpenCourseWare is an idea – and an ideal – developed by the MIT faculty who share the Institute's mission to advance knowledge and educate students in science, technology, and other areas of scholarship to best serve the world. In 1999, the Faculty considered how to use the Internet in pursuit of this goal, and in 2000 proposed OCW. MIT published the first proof-of-concept site in 2002, containing 50 courses. By November 2007, MIT completed the initial publication of virtually the entire curriculum, over 1,800 courses in 33 academic disciplines. Going forward, the OCW team is updating existing courses and adding new content and services to the site. (http://ocw.mit.edu/OcwWeb/web/about/history/index.htm)

OCW does not grant degrees nor provide access to faculty. Site statistics show that 49% of users are by self-learners, 32% by students and 16% by teachers. The OpenCourseWare Consortium[11]

> is a collaboration of more than 100 higher education institutions and associated organizations from around the world creating a broad and deep body of open educational content using a shared model. The mission of the OpenCourseWare Consortium is to advance education and empower people worldwide through opencourseware.

On November 28 2207 MIT celebrated the initial publication of the entire MIT curriculum on OpenCourseWare with a conference called Unlocking Knowledge, Empowering Minds with a keynote by Thomas Friedman and a symposium panel on the future of OCW and education with Harold Abelson (Moderator) Professor, Electrical Engineering and Computer Science, MIT, Charles Vest, President, National Academy of Engineering, President Emeritus, MIT, John Seely Brown. Former Chief Scientist, Xerox Corporation and Sam Pitroda Chairman, National Knowledge Commission, Government of India.[12] Steven Lerman, Dean for Graduate Students, MIT, in his presentation mentioned that MIT OpenCourseWare has reached 35 million people and another 14 million in translation.

MIT is of course only one example of the OpenCourseWare movement, an important player, but nevertheless, only one institution amongst many.[13] Most recently The Cape Town Open Education Declaration subtitled 'Unlocking the promise of open educational resources' arose from a meeting convened in September 2007. The declaration begins:

> We are on the cusp of a global revolution in teaching and learning. Educators worldwide are developing a vast pool of educational resources on the Internet, open and free for all to use. These educators are creating a world where each and every person on earth can access and contribute to the sum of all human knowledge. They are also planting the seeds of a new pedagogy where educators and learners create, shape and evolve knowledge together, deepening their skills and understanding as they go.

This emerging open education movement combines the established tradition of sharing good ideas with fellow educators and the collaborative, interactive culture of the Internet. It is built on the belief that everyone should have the freedom to use, customize, improve and redistribute educational resources without constraint. Educators, learners and others who share this belief are gathering together as part of a worldwide effort to make education both more accessible and more effective.

The Declaration mentions the expanding global collection of OCW as the basis for this development, although in terms of the history it is clear that origins and strands of the movement go back much further. The document also mentions the variety of openly licensed course materials, including lessons, games, software and other teaching and learning materials that contribute to making education more accessible and help shape and give effect to a 'participatory culture of learning, creating, sharing and cooperation' necessary for knowledge societies. Perhaps, most importantly, the Declaration indicates that open education 'is not limited to just open educational resources...[but] also draws upon open technologies that facilitate collaborative, flexible learning and the open sharing of teaching practices that empower educators to benefit from the best ideas of their colleagues. It goes on to provides a statement based on a three-pronged strategy designed to support 'open educational technology, open sharing of teaching practices and other approaches that promote the broader cause of open education.'[14]

The open education movement and paradigm has arrived. It emerges from a complex historical background and its futures are intimately tied not only to open source, open access and open publishing movements but also to the concept of the open society itself and its meanings.

THE EMERGING PARADIGM OF OPEN EDUCATION

What is now called simply 'open education' has emerged strongly as a new paradigm of social production in the global knowledge economy. In the last year or so four major reports have documented existing developments and new tools and technologies, heralded the utopian promise of 'openness' in global education extolling its virtues of shared commons-based peer-production and analyzed the ways in which it contributes to skill formation, innovation and economic development.

The powerful Washington-based Committee for Economic Development[15] released its report *Open Standards, Open Source, and Open Innovation: Harnessing the Benefits of Openness*[16] in April 2006 examining the phenomenon of 'openness' in the context of today's digital economy highlighting the key attributes of accessibility, responsiveness, and creativity and commenting on the relevance of three areas of open standards, open-source software, and open innovation. The report by The Digital Connections Council of The Committee For Economic Development built on three earlier reports dating from 2001: *The Digital Economy and Economic Growth* (2001), *Digital Economy: Promoting Competition, Innovation, and Opportunity* (2001) and *Promoting Innovation and Economic Growth: The Special Problem of Digital Intellectual Property* (2004).[17] These reports emphasized intellectual property issues involved with file-sharing and peer-to-peer networks and the way that 'heavy-handed enforcement of intellectual property rules and reliance on business practices designed for the trade of physical goods can stifle the collaboration and innovation that is vital to the growth of the digital economy.' What is perhaps of greatest interest in the present context is the emphasis in the new report on what they call 'open innovation' – new collaborative models of open innovation, originating outside the firm, that results in an 'architecture of participation' (Tim O'Reilly)—and to a lesser extent their definition of 'openness'. This is what the report says about 'open innovation':

> Open innovation can be seen in the growing use of digital software tools tied to computer-controlled fabrication devices that allow users to design an object and then produce it physically. As the costs of these digital design tools decrease, users are able to innovate, breaking the model of manufacturers being the source of innovation and customers simply consuming them. The openness model, the antithesis of a "not invented here" attitude, encompasses not only manufacturers and users, but suppliers whose innovations should be welcomed by the companies they supply. (Executive Summary).

The report goes on to mention 'the extraordinary increase in "peer production" of digital information products' which are produced by individuals without any expectation of monetary gain and commenting that 'sophisticated commercial firms are harvesting the benefits of openness.' In this same context they mention the movement of 'open science' promoted by the National Institutes of Health (NIH) and the model of open courseware on which they comment:

> Advocates for more openness contend that openness will result in greater innovation than would be achieved by restricting access to information or allowing first creators to exert greater control over it. Such a belief in the value of tapping the collective wisdom is profoundly democratic.

What is remarkable about this set of statements is the link between firm innovation, what we might all open education and the emergence of the paradigm of social production (more about this concept later).

In 2007 three substantial reports were released that reviewed open education as a movement and assessed its benefits: The OECD's (2007) *Giving Knowledge for*

Free: The Emergence Of Open Educational Resources[18]; Open e-Learning Content Observatory Services (OLCOS) project and report entitled *Open Educational Practices and Resources*[19]; *A Review of the Open Educational Resources (OER) Movement: Achievements, Challenges, and New Opportunities* (Eds. Atkins, Brown & Hammond, 2007), a report to The William and Flora Hewlett Foundation[20]. These three reports share similar emphases each focusing on 'openness' and the promise of the new technologies and their educational benefits. The OECD report focuses on four questions:

How can sustainable cost/benefit models for OER initiatives be developed?

What are the intellectual property rights issues linked to OER initiatives?

What are the incentives and barriers for universities and faculty staff to deliver their materials to OER initiatives?

How can access and usefulness for the users of OER initiatives be improved? (pp. 3–4, Foreword)

The Executive Summary gives us a flavor of the potential of OE[21] and the utopian educational promise that graces these three reports:

An apparently extraordinary trend is emerging. Although learning resources are often considered as key intellectual property in a competitive higher education world, more and more institutions and individuals are sharing digital learning resources over the Internet openly and without cost, as open educational resources (OER). (p. 9).

The report then concerns itself with the following questions: What are open educational resources? Who is using and producing OER and how much? Why are people sharing for free? What are the provisions for copyright and open licences? How can OER projects be sustained in the long run? alongside a set of policy implications and recommendations.

The OLCOS report, by comparison, focuses on: Policies, institutional frameworks and business models; Open Access and open content repositories; and Laboratories of open educational practices and resources, warning against instituting open education within the dominant model:

OER are understood to be an important element of policies that want to leverage education and lifelong learning for the knowledge economy and society. However, OLCOS emphasizes that it is crucial to also promote innovation and change in educational practices. In particular, OLCOS warns that delivering OER to the still dominant model of teacher centred knowledge transfer will have little effect on equipping teachers, students and workers with the competences, knowledge and skills to participate successfully in the knowledge economy and society. This report emphasises the need to foster open practices of teaching and learning that are informed by a competency-based educational framework. However, it is understood that a shift towards such practices will only happen in the longer term in a step-by-step process.

Bringing about this shift will require targeted and sustained efforts by educational leaders at all levels (p. 12).

In Chapter 4 'Competences for the knowledge society' the report opines 'priority must be given to open educational practices that involve students in active, constructive engagement with content, tools and services in the learning process, and promote learners' self-management, creativity and working in teams' (p. 37) and 'introduces the idea of value chains of open educational content which emerge when teachers and students re-use available content and make enriched and/or additional material (e.g. use cases, experiences, lessons learned, etc.) available again to a larger community of practice' (p. 37). The report defines a competency-focused, collaborative paradigm of learning and knowledge acquisition where 'priority is given to learning communities and development of knowledge and skills required for tackling and solving problems instead of subject-centred knowledge transfer.' The report argues:

> We believe that, to acquire the competences and skills for personal and professional achievement in the knowledge-based society, the learner's autonomy, personal mastery and self-direction must be acknowledged and innovative approaches implemented that foster self management, communication and team skills, and analytical, conceptual, creative and problem solving skills. However, there is of course a huge difference between identifying required competences and operationalising them for inclusion in the concrete practices of teaching and learning at different educational levels (p. 39).

The report then lists the following skills of 'digital competence'

> Ability to search, collect and process (create, organise, distinguish relevant from irrelevant, subjective from objective, real from virtual) electronic information, data and concepts and to use them in a systematic way;

> Ability to use appropriate aids (presentations, graphs, charts, maps) to produce, present or understand complex information;

> Ability to access and search a website and to use internet-based services such as discussion forums and e-mail;

> Ability to use ICT to support critical thinking, creativity and innovation in different contexts at home, leisure and work (p. 39).

The report to The William and Flora Hewlett Foundation is perhaps, the most comprehensive even although it follows similar lines of investigation to the others but frames the report in terms of Amartya Sen's work with the plan to develop 'a strategic international development initiative to expand people's substantive freedoms through the removal of "unfreedoms"'. What is impressive about this report is not only the inventory of open education projects (the incubation of high-quality specialized open resources) but also its attempt to conceptualize the issues and to move to a new understanding of openness in terms of an ethic of participation (and the design of 'open participatory learning infrastructure') that supports the role of technology in emphasizing the social nature of learning and its potential to address questions of the digital divide in developing countries.

There is much else that deserves attention in these reports. While they touch on conceptual issues to do with openness they do not often make the necessary theoretical links to the wider literature. They do not explore the concept of openness itself, nor investigate its history in the development of open systems. It is important to realize that today's 'open education' is not just a happy coincidence of technology and inclination, online learning and Web 2.0 technologies. Open education as an emergent paradigm has a history that provides much of the context and the motivating values. It is part of the Enlightenment story of freedom and it cannot be separated from wider political questions concerning epistemology, ontology and ethics.

NOTES

[1] See Peter Suber's blog at http://www.earlham.edu/~peters/fos/fosblog.html.
[2] See http://chronicle.com/news/article/3943/harvard-faculty-adopts-open-access-requirement.
[3] See the comment by Ray English on the same site.
[4] The Association of College and Research Libraries (ACRL) recently released their research agenda for scholarly publishing around eight themes: The impact and implications of cyberinfrastructure; Changing organizational models; How scholars work; Authorship and scholarly publishing; Value and value metrics of scholarly communications; Adoptions of successful innovations; Preservation of critical material Public policy and legal matters. See http://www.acrl.ala.org/scresearchagenda/index.php?title=Main_Page.
[5] See the website for the journal at http://www.wwwords.co.uk/pfie/index.asp
[6] See (2007) REVIEW SYMPOSIUM, Policy Futures in Education, 5(3), pp. 401–423 http://dx.doi.org/10.2304/pfie.2007.5.3.401
[7] Ubiquity magazine has received permission to publish an excerpt (Introduction and Chapter 11). The excerpt is available at http://www.acm.org/ubiquity/views/v8i18_peter.html. Ubiquity associate editor A. Triptahi writes of it: 'Prophetically, almost thirty years ago Jean-François Lyotard forecast the end of the modern research university based on Enlightenment principles. He envisaged the emergence of technical institutes in the service of the information-rich global multinationals. This book reflects on the post-war Western university and its discourses charting the crisis of the concept of the modern university. First, it examines the university within a global networked economy; second, it adopts poststructuralist perspectives in epistemology, politics and ethics to appraise the role of the contemporary university; third, it introduces the notion of 'development' in a critical fashion as a way of explaining its potentially new regional and international learning roles; fourth, it analyses the rise of global science and the disciplines in the context of the global economy; and, finally, it raises Lyotard's "logic of performativity" and the assessment of research quality within a neoliberal economy, linking it firmly to the question of freedom and the republic of science.
[8] See http://www.wun.ac.uk/cks/teaching/horizons/horizons.html for the six presentations in the series.
[9] This course, perhaps closest to the concerns of this paper, theorizes the emergent paradigm of Open Education (OE): 'first, by setting the scene briefly outlining the challenges of higher education represented by globalization, the knowledge economy and the development of e-learning; second, by reviewing and concept and contemporary forms of 'openness', including open source, open access and the 'open society'; third, by providing a grounding in the state of the field of open education, including related topics like copyright, licensing and sustainability; and, fourth, by encouraging innovation concerning current practices and possible alternative practices in open education' (Course description) .

[10] See, for example, the Indian Open Schooling Network (IOSN) at http://www.nos.org/iosn.htm, the National Institute of Open Schooling at http://www.nos.org/, and Open School BC (British Columbia) at http://www.pss.gov.bc.ca/osbc/.

[11] At http://www.ocwconsortium.org/index.php?option=com_content&task=view&id=15&Itemid=29

[12] The videos are available for viewing at http://ocw.mit.edu/OcwWeb/web/about/milestone/index.htm

[13] See the OpenCourseWare Consortium for the full list of participating countries and list of courses at http://www.ocwconsortium.org/

[14] The full declaration can be found at http://www.capetowndeclaration.org/read-the-declaration.

[15] See the website http://www.ced.org

[16] See http://www.ced.org/docs/report/report_ecom_openstandards.pdf

[17] Digital versions are available on their website at http://www.ced.org/projects/ecom.shtml

[18] Available electronically at http://www.oecd.org/document/41/0,3343,en_2649_201185_38659497_1_1_1_1,00.html

[19] Available at http://www.olcos.org/cms/upload/docs/olcos_roadmap.pdf

[20] Available at http://www.oerderves.org/wp-content/uploads/2007/03/a-review-of-the-open-educational-resources-oer-movement_final.pdf

[21] I prefer the term OE to OER because it embraces the notion of practices as well as the notion of sharing educational resources and also because it gels with open source, open access, and open science (as well as open innovation).

REFERENCES

Benkler, Y. (2006). *The wealth of networks: How social production.* New Haven, CT: Yale University Press.

Easthope, G. (1975). *Community, hierarchy and open education.* London: Routledge and Kegan Paul.

Illich, I. (1972). *Deschooling society.* Harmondsworth: Penguin.

Ithaka Report, The. (2007). University Publishing in a Digital Age, July 26, 2007, Laura Brown, Rebecca Griffiths, Matthew Rascoff, Preface: Kevin Guthrie. Retrieved from http://www.ithaka.org/strategicservices/Ithaka%20University%20Publishing%20Report.pdf

Kapitkze, C., & Peters, M. A. (2007). *Global knowledge cultures.* Rotterdam: Sense Publishers.

Materu, P. (2004). *Open source courseware: A baseline study.* Washington, DC: The World Bank.

Nyberg, D. (Ed.). (1975). *The philosophy of open education.* London: Routledge and Kegan Paul.

Peters, M. A., & Besley, A. C. (2006). *Building knowledge cultures: Education and development in the age of knowledge capitalism.* Lanham, MD; Boulder, CO; New York; Oxford: Rowman & Littlefield.

Peters, M. A. (2007a). *Knowledge economy, development and the future of higher education: Reclaiming the cultural mission.* Rotterdam: Sense Publishers.

Peters, M. A. (2007b). Opening the book (From the closed to the open text). *The International Journal of the Book, 5*(1), 77–84. Retrieved from http://ijb.cgpublisher.com/product/pub.27/prod.199

Rogers, C. (1969). *Freedom to learn: A view of what education might become* (1st ed.). Columbus, OH: Charles Merill.

Willinski, J. (2006). *The access principle: The case for open access to research and scholarship.* Cambridge, MA: MIT Press.

Michael A. Peters
Department of Educational Policy Studies,
University of Illinois at Urbana-Champaign

DANIEL ARAYA

2. THE DEMOCRATIC TURN

Prosumer Innovation and Learning in the Knowledge Economy

INTRODUCTION

As Eric Von Hippel (2005) has pointed out, the distributed nature of information and communications technologies is enabling an emergent mode of economic production that is best described as "democratic innovation". Looking at democratic innovation from the perspective of complexity theory, I will suggest that the nature of socioeconomic production is becoming increasingly anchored to "prosumer innovation" networks. Building out from information and communications networks (ICNs), prosumer innovation blurs the boundaries between producers and consumers, joining both categories to broader systems of creative cooperation. This chapter will explore the contours of prosumer innovation and consider its potential for advancing systems of education. Focusing on prosumer innovation as an emergent cultural practice, I will suggest that the democratization of knowledge and learning should be the locus of concern for educational policy-makers over the coming decades.

THE DEMOCRATIC TURN: ICNS AND CULTURAL PRODUCTION

Over the past quarter century, policy discourse in advanced capitalist countries has increasingly focused on the economic needs associated with the production of knowledge. Unlike the tangible assets linked to the industrial economy- land, labor, capital, and raw materials, the knowledge economy is largely defined by abstract goods such as research, creativity, design, innovation, and learning. For theorists like Alvin Toffler (1990) and Peter Drucker (1993), the knowledge economy represents a socioeconomic shift from labour-intensive "smokestack industries" to "mind work".

Impacting the global economy in varied ways, knowledge and innovation are becoming central to commercial production. From network-driven business services and automated production systems, to complex engineering and just-in-time manufacturing, the knowledge economy is characterized as a new mode of capitalist production (Castells 1996; Womack et al., 1991). This is not to say that industrial manufacturing is disappearing (as if that were possible), but that technology and innovation are becoming the dominant forces of economic growth. Put differently, while Fordist manufacturing is maintained as a necessary component of production, it no longer serves as the economic engine.

M.A. Peters and R.G. Britez (eds.), Open Education and Education for Openness, 17–31.

Much as the assembly line shifted the critical factor of production from labor to capital, today the computer is shifting the critical factor of production from capital to innovation. Underlying this socioeconomic restructuring is the emerging importance of information and communications networks (ICNs). Beyond the command-and-control production systems characteristic of Fordist production, networks have become infrastructural to global systems of production. As Manuel Castells (2004) observes,

> Networked organisations [now] outcompete all other forms of organisation, particularly the vertical, rigid, command-and-control bureaucracies... Companies that do not or cannot follow this logic are outperformed and ultimately phased out by leaner, more flexible competitors. (p. 222)

Along with changes in the management of production, information networks are giving rise to new modes of socioeconomic collaboration. Moving beyond the simple "one-to-many" linear model of industrial manufacturing, ICNs are making possible "many-to-many" production. In his book *The Wealth of Networks* (2006), Yochai Benkler describes this new economic model as "commons-based peer production". Highlighting a wide range of examples including Wikipedia and open source software (OSS), Benkler suggests that information networks have enabled a third mode of production- beyond both the state and capital market. For Benkler, the key to understanding this emergent socioeconomic practice is the capacity of distributed networks to facilitate open source innovation. Put in the simplest terms, open source innovation is the organization of complex production through the coordination of self-organizing social networks. While traditional systems of production leverage closed proprietary systems, commons-based production utilizes open networks as platforms to harness the creative energy of volunteer contributors. Wikipedia, for example, now has more than 2.5 million articles in several languages and has become the largest encyclopedia in the world.

While peer production may depend upon the technological capacity of networks, it is ultimately configured by an emergent socio-political structure grounded in peer-to-peer (P2P) collaboration. What makes P2P so different from other modes of production is that it doesn't rely on monetary incentives or fixed hierarchical organization. No single entity "owns" the product or manages its direction. In peer projects like social networking and OSS, for example, resources are contributed spontaneously. Political authority is "organic", emerging and receding with the domain-based expertise needed to complete specific tasks. In these democratic "production ecologies", authority does not disappear, but neither does it cohere in permanent socio-political hierarchies. P2P collaboration is literally production that is dependent upon the *voluntary participation of partners* (Bauwens, 2005).

PROSUMER INNOVATION AND P2P COLLABORATION

In their book *Wikinomics* (2006), Don Tapscott and Anthony Williams explore the potential of peer production for advancing business enterprise. As they observe, the emerging consensus is that business models that are based on mass production are slowly being eclipsed by new models based on mass collaboration:

> Throughout history corporations have organized themselves according to strict hierarchical lines of authority. Everyone was a subordinate to someone else— employees versus managers, marketers versus customers, producers versus supply chain subcontractors, companies versus the community. There was always someone or some company in charge, controlling things, at the "top" of the food chain. While hierarchies are not vanishing, profound changes in the nature of technology, demographics, and the global economy are giving rise to powerful new models of production based on community, collaboration, and self-organization rather than on hierarchy and control. (p. 1)

Tapscott and Williams make a compelling case for *prosumer innovation* as a significant new business strategy. Originally coined by Alvin Toffler (1980), prosumer innovation blurs the boundaries between consumers and producers, joining both categories to broader socioeconomic networks of creative collaboration. According to Tapscott and Williams, mass collaboration is a direct consequence of networks as platforms for innovation. Using examples ranging from software, music, publishing, and pharmaceuticals, Tapscott and Williams link P2P-driven web services like MySpace, InnoCentive, flickr, Second Life and YouTube to the rising power of prosumer-driven innovation. In the online virtual world *Second Life*, for example, prosumers form broad user-communities that create rich value-added products and services that are not possible within traditional business models.

Open business models like Second Life invite customers to add value by offering a platform for creativity. Tapscott and Williams point out that technologies like Apple's iPod and Sony's PSP are now routinely "hacked" to enable creative changes in their design and performance: "Whether it's modifying the casing, installing custom software, or...doubling the memory, users are transforming the ubiquitous music and media player[s] into something unique" (p. 133).

The rising influence of prosumer hacking is the result of a convergence of P2P networks and user-friendly editing tools. Whiles consumers with the skills and inclination to hack commercial products like the iPod remain a minority, they are a growing consumer demographic. Rather than fighting this rising tide, Tapscott and Williams argue that companies should begin to harness these changes by bringing customers into their business webs and giving them lead roles in next-generation products and services:

> Forget about static, immovable products. If your customers are going to treat products as platforms anyway, then you may as well be ahead of the game. Make your products modular, reconfigurable, and editable. Set the context for customer innovation and collaboration. Provide venues. Build user-friendly customer tool kits. Supply the raw materials that customers need to add value to your product. Make it easy to remix and share. We call this designing for prosumption. (p. 148)

As they point out, it may be true that prosumer hacking forces a company to risk losing control of its product platform, but it is also true that "a company that fights its users risks soiling its reputation by shutting out potentially valuable sources of innovation" (pp. 135–6). As Tapscott and Williams observe, prosumer innovation works because it leverages self-organization as a mode of production. In their view, business leaders that want to tap this creative potential must begin to understand the needs and interests of this new market.

DEMOCRATIC INNOVATION AND DESIGN

In his book *Democratizing Innovation* (2005) Eric Von Hippel adds another critical layer to understanding prosumer innovation. Exploring the democratization of innovation in the context of design, Von Hippel argues that user-centered innovation represents the next mode of design-based manufacturing. He writes,

> When I say that innovation is becoming democratized, I mean that users of products and services- both firms and individual consumers- are increasingly able to innovate for themselves. User-centered innovation processes offer great advantages over manufacturer centric innovation development systems that have been the mainstay of commerce for hundreds of years. Users that innovate can develop exactly what they want, rather than relying on manu-facturers to act as their (often very imperfect) agents. Moreover, individual users do not have to develop everything they need on their own: they can benefit from innovations developed and freely shared by others. (p. 1)

While traditional interpretations of innovation are focused on manufacturers as lead designers for mass consumption, Von Hippel argues that "a growing body of empirical work shows that users are [becoming] the first to develop many and perhaps most new industrial and consumer products". Using examples from wide ranging industries including sports equipment, software development and food services, Von Hippel argues that the contribution of product users to design is growing steadily larger as a result of emerging technologies:

> It is becoming progressively easier for many users to get precisely what they want by designing it for themselves. And innovation by users appears to increase social welfare. At the same time, the ongoing shift of product-development activities from manufacturers to users is painful and difficult for many manufacturers. Open, distributed innovation is "attacking" a major structure of the social division of labor. Many firms and industries must make fundamental changes to long-held business models in order to adapt. (pp. 2–3)

As Von Hippel observes, one major difference between users and manufacturers is *context*: While manufacturers largely rely on iterative improvements to well-established product designs, user-innovators tend to develop novel designs better suited to their unique environments. In turn, this practice of situated creativity is augmented further by the fact that prosumer-innovators often "freely reveal" their designs. As he explains, in order to leverage their creative efforts, prosumers often rely on open collaboration and shared invention. Spontaneously forming communities-of-practice (Wenger, 1998), prosumer-innovators share information in order to continually distribute the creative load. As Von Hippel elaborates, this has become increasingly easier with the affordances of ICNs:

> User's ability to innovate is improving radically and rapidly as a result of the steadily improving quality of computer software and hardware, improved access to easy-to-use tools and components for innovation, and access to a steadily richer innovation commons. Today user firms and individual hobbyists have access to sophisticated programming tools for software and sophisticated CAD design tools for hardware and electronics. These information-based tools can be run on a personal computer, and they are rapidly coming down in price. As a consequence, innovation by users will continue to grow even if the degree of heterogeneity of need and willingness to invest in obtaining a precisely right product remains constant. (p. 13)

Since manufacturing firms still have advantages of scale over distributed clusters of heterogeneous user-innovators, Von Hippel advises commercial firms to develop tool-kits to allow prosumers to design and customize products and components. As he points out, this is already the case in many industries. In the semiconductor industry for example, billions of dollars worth of semiconductors are designed and produced using user tool-kits every year (p. 16). Neither is it new for user-hobbyists to have specialized tools for "amateur" work in areas such as home improvement, carpentry or software development. What is new however, is the direct linking of manufacturers to users so that custom designs can ultimately be manufactured "as is".

The use of tool-kits and the consequent democratization of innovation, reflects a larger capacity emerging with ICNs in the knowledge economy, a capacity that will very likely transform contemporary modes of education and learning.

PROSUMER INNOVATION AND EDUCATION

But what precisely is the role of institutional education in era increasingly dominated by technologies that support democratic collaboration? In their article "Minds on Fire" (2008), John Seely Brown and Richard Adler attempt to answer this very question by considering the educational potential of social networks. Just as peer communities are transforming the production of software, Brown and Adler speculate that social learning communities will transform the production of education. As they observe, the Internet and related network technologies are enabling a revolution in social learning that is interdependent with highly distributed communities-of-practice. Unlike the traditional Cartesian approach centered on the individual learner, social learning networks depend upon highly developed forms of community apprenticeship:

> In a traditional Cartesian educational system, students may spend years learning about a subject; only after amassing sufficient (explicit) knowledge are they expected to start acquiring the (tacit) knowledge or practice of how

to be an active practitioner/professional in a field. But viewing learning as the process of joining a community of practice reverses this pattern and allows new students to engage in "learning to be" even as they are mastering the content of a field. This encourages the practice of what John Dewey called "productive inquiry"—that is, the process of seeking the knowledge when it is needed in order to carry out a particular situated task. (p. 20)

Brown and Adler connect this communities-of-practice approach to a larger shift in institutional education itself. Just as prosumers are collaborating across distributed networks to create dynamic products and services, they contend that the future of education lies in opening up the design and development of courseware and curriculum to peer production. As they observe,

> We need to construct shared, distributed, reflective practicums in which experiences are collected, vetted, clustered, commented on, and tried out in new contexts. One might call this "learning about learning," a bootstrapping operation in which educators, along with students, are learning among and between themselves. (p. 28)

For Brown and Adler, this is education as "passion-based" learning in which students become apprentices in self-organizing social networks. Underlying this communities-of-practice model is a resource-driven understanding of education in which the World Wide Web represents a rich storehouse of tools and resources for ongoing cultural innovation. This knowledge commons includes open courseware and access to powerful simulation models, as well as open access to scholarly websites and journals. They write:

> This new form of learning begins with the knowledge and practices acquired in school but is equally suited for continuous, lifelong learning that extends beyond formal schooling. Indeed, such an environment might encourage students to readily and happily pick up new knowledge and skills as the world shifts beneath them. (p. 32)

CONNEXIONS: DEMOCRATIZING THE KNOWLEDGE COMMONS

One clear example of what Brown and Adler are exploring is the *Connexions* project at Rice University. Launched in 1999, Connexions is a cross-disciplinary knowledge commons that fosters the ongoing construction of tools and resources for all levels of education (Connexions White Paper, 2004). Inspired by the tremendous growth of open-source software, Connexions is designed to offer students and educators access to modular resources from around the world. Authors contributing to Connexions retain copyright on all resources but make them freely available under a *Creative Commons* license.

As a resource repository, Connexions is constructed as a globally-distributed environment that transcends the exclusivity of classroom knowledge transmission. While knowledge is traditionally transmitted to students in highly formalized stages, Connexions offers students the possibility to access the knowledge continuum in its entirety. Using a P2P architecture, Connexions operates as a single, nonlinear network that can enable students and researchers to enter into the knowledge continuum from any point of interest. Most importantly, by giving anyone access to the entire continuum, Connexions encourages students and teachers to perceive the "big picture" of knowledge in a holistic way:

> The traditional method of transmitting this information- textbook publishing- is inefficient. In contrast to the rate at which the knowledge continuum changes, it is a glacial process. The dynamics of the system are lost; students receive what is essentially a still photograph of the continuum at a given point in time. Textbook authors must devote several years to writing their books, and then their work is subject to editorial review. Finally their books enter the printing and marketing cycle. This is a substantial time commitment for college professors. Thus, textbooks are, almost by definition, stale even at the date of their publication. Knowledge that is evolving at a rapid pace, such as in computer science, environmental science, bioinformatics, and medicine, can never be captured by this traditional delivery method. (Connexions 2004, p. 3)

Designed around an open-content license, Connexions supports a globally inclusive authoring environment for teachers, researchers and students. Authors can build on and advance anything in the *Content Commons*. While educational modules are encoded in a single language (XML), modules can be translated into a number of media formats including HTML, PostScript, PDF, Microsoft Word and PowerPoint. Moreover, modular units stored in the Commons can be combined and used in an infinite variety of courseware packages.

The collaborative nature of Connexions fuses participatory feedback to iterative improvement in the ongoing expansion of the repository. In this way, Connexions facilitates self-organizing prosumer improvement without limiting access. Using visualization and navigational tools, curriculum developers can continually mine a rich repository of highly scalable resources. In turn, using post-publication editorial and review, specialists can utilize independent standards to harvest quality materials suitable to domain specific needs. Moreover, third party editorial boards can employ independent lenses to filter and manage the raw resources as needed.

Available free of charge to anyone under an open-content license, Connexions aims to enable a large-scale repository for global learning communities. While the Content Commons repository remains technologically centralized, the goal of Connexions is to grow its' infrastructure along with its reach in order to enable a truly globally-distributed P2P ecosystem. Deliberately designed to support global collaboration, Connexions is a concrete example of a distributed network supporting prosumer communities. In this regard, Connexions represents a strong model of the tremendous scalability of collaborative networks to facilitate user-driven learning. More to the point, as a knowledge commons, Connexions offers a comprehensive framework for considering the development of educational tools and resources for democratic innovation.

COMPLEXITY: UNDERSTANDING PEER PRODUCTION

Fundamental to this democratic shift is an emerging understanding that networks offer a robust platform for shared collaboration and learning-by-doing. To understand the underlying dynamism of network production, however, we must begin by exploring complex living systems.

The concept of the network was developed in the 1920s to describe communities of organisms linked through food webs and its use then became extended to all systems levels: cells as networks of molecules; organisms as networks of cells; ecosystems as networks of individual organisms (Capra, 1996; Barabasi, 2002). The network pattern is one of the very basic patterns of organization of all living systems whose key characteristic is self-generation—the continual production, reproduction, repair and regeneration of the network.

Unlike machines, living systems have no controlling parts or levels. While biologists once viewed natural systems in mechanistic terms, many scientists now study living systems in terms of complex networks. Since living organisms rely on an interdependence of "communication" between component parts, they are not easily reduced to hierarchies of command-and-control. As the parts of an organism adjust and respond to the changes required for maintenance, the whole is preserved as an integral unit. Ervin Laszlo (2001) explains it this way,

> The concept "the whole is more than the sum of its parts" holds, for when the parts are integrated within the living organism, properties emerge and processes take place that are not the simple sum of the properties or aggregate of the processes of the parts. The living organism can not be reduced to the interaction of its parts without losing its "emergent properties"- the very characteristics that make it living. (p. 180)

One major key to understanding natural systems is their capacity for "autopoiesis" or self-production (Varela and Maturana 1974). Systems in nature are not constrained by entropy but function as "open systems", capable of exchanging matter and energy with their environment. In the context of natural science, an open system is any system with borders that are permeable to both energy and mass. Where closed systems contain limited energy and are vulnerable to entropy, open systems can tap a potentially infinite supply of energy from the surrounding environment. By "importing" energy across permeable boundaries, open systems absorb the resources necessary for self-creation. It is this capacity for "bottom-up" self-organization that enables living systems to evolve. As we are coming to understand, it is this very capacity that helps explain contemporary changes in economic production as well.

By importing volunteer labor across organizational boundaries, prosumer innovation systems are not constrained by cultural entropy but are continually replenished. Put differently, it is precisely the open structure of peer systems that stokes continuous innovation.

PEER PRODUCTION: FROM HIERARCHY TO HETERARCHY

As an emergent mode of production, peer production not only "flattens" the organizational pyramid it creates an ecology-of-exchange without recourse to higher authority at all. Ironically, it is this very quality that makes prosumer innovation so attractive to commercial organizations. Internet companies like *Amazon* and *Ebay*, for example, have produced compelling business models by directly integrating prosumer participation into their service structures.

Peer networks represent an emergent mode of human socio-political organization highly conducive to creativity and innovation. P2P networks such as the World Wide Web, for example, capitalize on "heterarchical" systems of organization. Unlike the top-down structures that are critical to industrial production, heterarchical systems depend upon the isomorphic structure of networks. While definitions of the word heterarchy vary, heterarchical structures are generally defined as networks of elements that share the same "horizontal" position of power and authority. In P2P computer networks, for example, an infinite density of point-to-point connections enable any computer node to connect to any other without the need for mediation (the Internet being the most obvious example of this).

Over the course of history, hierarchical organization has been a central technology for managing economic, social and political development. Loosely defined, a hierarchy is a vertical system of ranking and organizing in which each component element is subordinate to another in a descending ladder or pyramid. The fact that hierarchies have been the central medium for managing human affairs throughout most of human history is testament to their utility. Today, however, as the center of production shifts away from management and towards creativity and innovation, the value of hierarchical organization is now in doubt:

> Throughout most of human history, hierarchies of one form or another have served as the primary engines of wealth creation and provided a model for institutions such as the church, the military, and government. So pervasive and enduring has the hierarchical mode of organization been that most people assume that there are no viable alternatives. Whether the ancient slave empires of Greece, Rome, China, and the Americas, the feudal kingdoms that later covered the planet, or the capitalist corporation, hierarchies have organized people into layers of superiors and subordinates to fulfill both public and private objectives. Even the management literature today that advocates empowerment, teams and enlightened management techniques takes as a basic premise the command modus operandi inherent in the modern corporation. Though it is unlikely that hierarchies will disappear in the foreseeable future, a new form of horizontal organization is emerging that rivals the hierarchical firm in its capacity to create information-based products and services, and in some cases, physical things. (Tapscott and Williams, p. 23)

COLLECTIVE INTELLIGENCE AND PROSUMER INNOVATION

The Internet represents a global sociotechnological platform in which the knowledge, resources, and computing power of billions of people are increasingly coming together into a massive collective force:

> Energized through blogs, wikis, chat rooms, personal broadcasting, and other forms of peer-to-peer creation and communication, this utterly decentralized and amorphous force increasingly self-organizes to provide its own news, entertainment, and services. As these effects permeate out through the economy and intersect with deep structural changes like globalization, we will witness the rise of an entirely new kind of economy where firms coexist with millions of autonomous producers who connect and cocreate value in loosely coupled networks. (Tapscott and Williams, p. 32)

Perhaps one of the most ambitious attempts to consider the implications of mass collaboration is Pierre Lévy's (1997) work in "collective intelligence". For Lévy, collective intelligence underlies a new paradigm that is emerging in various fields of research simultaneously,

> Far from being exclusive, the expression "collective intelligence" relates to an extensive body of knowledge and thoughts concerned with several objects that have been diversely labeled: distributed cognition, distributed knowledge systems, global brain, super-brain, global mind, group mind, ecology of mind, hive mind, learning organization, connected intelligence, networked intelligence, augmented intelligence, hyper-cortex, symbiotic man, etc. Not withstanding their diversity, these several rich philosophical and scientific contemporary trends have one feature in common: they describe human communities, organizations and cultures exhibiting "mind-like" properties...

Lévy argues that a global civilization built around collective cultural production is emerging around ICNs. Beyond the fading superstructure of mass industrial society, Lévy believes that ICNs are giving birth to an age of shared cultural production. As he suggests,

> Those who manufacture things will become scarcer and scarcer, and their labour will become mechanized, augmented, automated to a greater and greater extent. Information processing skills will no longer be needed, for intelligent networks will soon be able to function with little human assistance. The final frontier will be the human itself, that which can't be automated: the creation of sensible worlds, invention, relation, the continuous creation of the community. (Lévy, 1997, p. 34)

The challenges of this new era are becoming obvious. The rapid evolution of technology has begun to displace the traditional social bonds of virtually every community in the world. Lévy argues that the urgent need for social cohesion will spawn the foundations for an economy increasingly built on a shared global culture. As the global economy progressively moves beyond goods and services, issues of ethics and shared human development become critical. Success in this cultural economy argues Lévy, is becoming contingent on a collaborative and evolving consciousness. He explains,

> A vast political and cultural plain stands before us. We have an opportunity to experience one of those rare moments when a civilization deliberately invents itself. But this opportunity won't last for long. Before blindly stumbling into a future from which we cannot return, it is essential that we begin to imagine, experiment with, and actively promote, within this new [informational] space, organizational structures and decision-making styles that are oriented toward a deepening of our sense of democracy. Cyberspace could become the most perfectly integrated medium within a community for problem analysis, group discussion, the development of an awareness of complex processes, collective decision-making, and evaluation. (p. 59)

Information technology represents a quantum jump in cognitive evolution. With the emergence of ICNs, the work of cultural construction is increasingly being supported by platforms that scaffold creative collaboration. For thinkers like Lévy, the World Wide Web represents the emergence of a semantic commons that is gradually enabling the whole of humanity to house and manage its cultural heritage. This is significant because it means that much of the world's knowledge may one day be available to be seen, explored and advanced by people throughout the world. Lévy describes this emerging democratic knowledge space as a virtual cosmopedia:

> Not only does the cosmopedia make available to the collective intellect all of the pertinent knowledge available to it at any given moment, but it also serves as a site of collective discussion, negotiation, and development. A pluralistic image of knowledge, the cosmopedia is the mediating fabric between the collective intellect and its world, between the collective intellect and itself. Knowledge is no longer separated from the concrete realizations that give it meaning, nor from the activities and practices that engender knowledge and that knowledge modifies in turn. Depending on the zones of use and paths of exploration, hierarchies between users and designers are inverted. A person who decides to learn about a topic in biochemistry or the history of art will be capable of supplying new information about a given sector of electronics or infant care, one in which he or she happens to specialize. In the cosmopedia all reading is writing... Unanswered questions within cosmopedic space, [will indicate] regions where invention and innovation are required. (pp. 217–8)

COLLECTIVE CULTURAL COGNITION

For sociocultural theorists, human cognition is mediated by embedded cultural practices that acquire meaning in social contexts. In this sense, human cognition is largely indistinguishable from the ongoing social practices of cultures and communities. Advancing on Lev Vygotsky (1978), sociocultural researchers contend that the internalization of cultural artifacts such as language, writing, and numbers, form the foundations for human consciousness:

> [T]here is reason to suspect that what we call cognition is in fact a complex social phenomenon. The point is not so much that arrangements of knowledge in the head correspond in a complicated way to the social world outside the head, but that they are socially organized in such a fashion as to be indivisible. 'Cognition' observed in everyday practice is distributed – stretched over, not divided among – mind, body, activity and culturally organized settings. (Lave, 1988, p. 1)

For sociocultural theorists, whole systems of artifacts (words and numbers) form the basic foundations for shared cultural cognition. For this reason, the construction of new cultural resources is highly dependent upon the mediated collaboration and evolution of cognitive tools. Just as new tools of labor facilitate new social structures, new tools of thinking facilitate new cognitive structures. This artifact-mediated understanding of human culture and consciousness is even more obvious today. With the emergence of worldwide ICNs, the process of knowledge construction is becoming highly dependent upon distributed communities-of-practice.

DEMOCRACY AND EDUCATION IN A KNOWLEDGE AGE

It is becoming clear that the application of ICNs to systems of knowledge and learning will be anchored to collaborative innovation. ICNs make possible a multimodal approach to learning systems that increasingly provides users with more and greater control over their own learning. As Lévy points out, this reflects an emergent global process grounded in collective intelligence. What is perhaps most fundamental to this new mode of production, however, is its' capacity to support prosumer innovation. This will very likely have revolutionary implications for institutional education. For this reason, it is critical that educators and educational policy makers begin to explore the possibilities and challenges of students as prosumer-innovators.

At the same time, the significant economic, technological and social changes emerging within a knowledge economy require that formal education redefine its' underlying assumptions. For educationalists like Bereiter (2002) and Scardamalia (2002), education in a knowledge economy is inherently linked to the capacity of all students to advance knowledge and ideas. They suggest that the health and wealth of societies depends increasingly on leveraging creativity. For this reason, Bereiter and Scardamalia suggest that the creative construction of new theories and ideas is the key to reshaping education. While traditionally, education systems have been constructed to support cultural reproduction, they have not given students the experience of independent idea improvement. As Bereiter and Scardamalia point out, people in general and not just a specialized elite need to be able to work creatively in the production of knowledge. What this means is that students of all ages must be directly engaged in the creation process.

As Bereiter and Scardamalia observe, the key to unlocking this potential is developing education as "knowledge building". This means fostering democratic communities around a shared knowledge commons. By connecting specialized communities to a shared environment, knowledge building can potentially enable cross-pollination and continuous idea improvement. As they point out, it is not enough to simply require students to master the component skills of knowledge creation: critical thinking, the scientific method, etc. The technological, social and ethical needs of a rapidly globalizing society will require people that can creatively construct and evolve new tools, ideas and practices. While pedagogy for mass education largely aimed at student mastery of established knowledge, education in a knowledge economy must work to scaffold creativity itself. Through the process of building knowledge collaboratively, students can achieve epistemic agency- that is, share in a cooperative effort for making knowledge innovation successful and of benefit to all.

As Bereiter and Scardamalia point out, a conservative bias within the structure of mass education has reduced knowledge creation to an elite few. The fact that it is only at the graduate level that students are actively encouraged to create knowledge is now becoming a significant problem. If knowledge innovation is to genuinely constitute the foundations of a knowledge economy, then public education must begin to move beyond social reproduction. This represents a challenge for institutional education but projects like Connexions demonstrate that a transformation in education is very likely already under way.

CONCLUSION

This chapter has explored the contours of prosumer innovation and its emerging potential for advancing social and economic production in the knowledge economy. Building out from new technologies, prosumer innovation is anchored to open systems and open networks of mass collaboration. Looking at prosumer innovation from the perspective of complex networks, I have considered the implications of this emerging cultural practice for systems of education. Focusing on collective intelligence and the democratization of knowledge creation, I have argued that prosumer innovation should now be a central area of exploration for theorists and practitioners in the field of educational policy.

REFERENCES

Albrow, M. (1997). *The global age*. Stanford, CA: Stanford University Press.
Amin, A. (1997). Post-fordism: Models, fantasies and phantoms of transition. In A. Amin (Ed.), *Post-fordism: A reader*. Cambridge: Blackwell Publishers Ltd.
Barabasi, A.-L. (2002). *Linked: The new science of networks*. New York: Perseus Publishing.
Bauwens, M. (2005). *P2P and human evolution*. Retrieved November 1, 2005, from http://www.networkcultures.org/weblog/archives/2005/03/michael_bauwens.html
Beck, U. (1999). *What is globalization?* Cambridge: Polity Press.
Beck, U. (2002). The cosmopolitanism society and its enemies. *Theory, Culture and Society, 19*, 17–44.
Becker, G. (1964). *Human capital*. Chicago: University of Chicago Press.

Bell, D. (1973). *The coming of post-industrial society*. New York: Basic Books.

Benkler, Y. (2006). *The wealth of networks: How social production transforms markets and freedom*. New Haven, CT: Yale University Press.

Bereiter, C. (2002). *Education and mind in the knowledge age*. Mahwah, NJ: Lawrence Erlbaum Associates.

Berman, K., & Annexstein, F. (2000). *A future educational tool for the 21st century: Peer-to-Peer computing*. Retrieved November 1, 2005, from http://www.ececs.uc.edu/~annexste/Papers/EduP2P.pdf

Brown, J. S., & Adler, R. (2008, January/Feburary). Minds on fire: Open education, the long tail, and learning 2.0. *Educause Review, 43*, 1.

Capra, F. (1996). *The web of life*. London: HarperCollins.

Capra, F. (2002). Living networks. In H. McCarthy, P. Miller, & P. Skidmore (Eds.), *Network logic: Who governs in an interconnected world?* Retrieved August 19, 2005, from http://www.demos.co.uk/files/File/networklogic02capra.pdf

Castells, M. (1996). *The rise of the networked society*. Oxford: Blackwell.

Connexions white paper. (2004). Rice University.

Dewey, J. (1997). *Democracy and education: An introduction to the philosophy of education*. New York: Simon and Schuster.

Drucker, P. (1993). *Post-capitalist society*. Oxford: Butterworth-Heinema.

Dyer-Witheford, N. (2000). *Cyber-Marx: Cycles and circuits of struggle in high-technology capitalism*. Chicago: University of Illinois Press.

Foray, D. (2004). *Economics of knowledge*. MIT Press.

Giroux, H. A. (2001). Critical education or training: Beyond the commodification of higher education. In H. A. Giroux & K. Myrsiades (Eds.), *Beyond the corporate university culture and pedagogy in the new millennium*. Lanham, MD: Rowman & Littlefield Publishers.

Halal, W. (1998). *The new management*. San Francisco: Berrett-Koehler.

Hardt, M., & Negri, A. (2000). *Empire*. Cambridge, MA: Harvard University Press.

Held, D., McGrew, A., Goldblatt, D., & Perraton, J. (1999). *Global transformations – Politics, economics and culture*. Cambridge: Polity Press.

Higher ed., inc. (2005, September 10). *The Economist, 376*(8443), 19–20.

Hilsenrath, J., & Buckman, R. (2003, October 20). The economy: Factory employment is falling worldwide; Study of 20 big economies finds 22 million jobs lost; Even China shows decline. *Wall Street Journal*, p. A2.

Huntington, S. (1996). *The clash of civilizations and the remaking of world order*. New York: Simon and Schuster.

Husén, T. (1974). *The learning society*. London: Methuen.

Husén, T. (1986). *The learning society revisited*. Oxford: Pergamon.

Hutchins, R. M. (1970). *The learning society*. Harmondsworth: Penguin.

Kauffman, S. (1996). *At home in the universe*. New York: Oxford University Press.

Kukla, A. (2000). *Social constructivism and the philosophy of science*. London: Routledge.

Laszlo, E. (1987). *Evolution: The grand synthesis*. Boston: Shambhala.

Laszlo, E. (1996). *The systems view of the world: A holistic vision for our time*. Cresskill, NJ: Hampton Press.

Laszlo, E. (2001). *Macroshift: Navigating the transformation to a sustainable world*. San Francisco: Berrett-Koehler.

Lave, J. (1988). *Cognition in practice*. Cambridge, UK: Cambridge University Press.

Lave, J., & Wenger, E. (1991). *Situated learning: Legitimate peripheral participation*. New York: Cambridge University Press.

Leadbeater, C. (2000). *Living on thin air: The new economy*. London: Penguin.

Lenski, G., Nolan, P., & Lenski, J. (1995). *Human societies: An introduction to macrosociology* (7th ed.). New York: McGraw-Hill.

Lévy, P. (1997). *Collective intelligence: Mankind's emerging world in cyberspace*. New York: Plenium Press.

LionShare White Paper. (2004). *Connecting and extending Peer-to-Peer networks: LionShare white paper*. Retrieved November 1, 2005, from http://lionshare.its.psu.edu/main/info/docspresentation/LionShareWP.pdf

Livingstone, D. (1999). *The education-jobs gap: Underemployment or economic democracy*. Toronto: Garamond Press.

Lyotard, J. (1984). *The post-modern condition: A report on knowledge* (G. Bennington & B. Massumi, Trans.). Minneapolis, MN: University of Minnesota Press.

Peters, M., & Besley, A. C. (2006). *Building knowledge cultures: Education and development in the age of knowledge capitalism*. Oxford: Rowman and Littlefield Publishers.

Readings, B. (1996). *The university in ruins*. Cambridge, MA: Harvard University Press.

Reich, R. (2000). *The future of success: Working and living in the new economy*. New York: Alfred A. Knopf.

Rifkin, J. (1995, October). Vanishing jobs. *Mother Jones*. Retrieved April 15, 2006, from http://www.motherjones.com/commentary/columns/1995/09/rifkin.html

Rifkin, J. (2000). *The age of access*. New York: Jeremy P. Tarcher/Putnam.

Robertson, R. (1992). *Globalization: Social theory and global culture*. London: Sage.

Scardamalia, M. (2002). Collective cognitive responsibility for the advancement of knowledge. In B. Smith (Ed.), *Liberal education in a knowledge society* (pp. 67–98). Chicago: Open Court.

Slaughter, S., & Leslie, L. (1997). *Academic capitalism: Politics, policies and the entrepreneurial university*. Baltimore: Johns Hopkins University Press.

Slaughter, S., & Rhoades, G. (2004). *Academic capitalism and the new economy: Markets, state and higher education*. Baltimore: Johns Hopkins University Press.

The brains business. (2005, September 10). *The Economist, 376*(8443), 3–5.

Tapscott, D. (1996). *The digital economy: Promise and peril in the age of networked intelligence*. New York: McGraw-Hill.

Tapscott, D., & Williams, A. (2006). *Wikinomics: How mass collaboration changes everything*. New York: Portfolio.

Toffler, A. (1980). *The third wave*. New York: Bantam Books.

Toffler, A. (1990). *Powershift: Knowledge, wealth and violence at the edge of the 21st century*. New York: Bantam Books.

Varela, F., Maturana, H., & Uribe, R. (1974). Autopoiesis: the organization of living systems, its characterization and a model. *Biosystems, 5*, 187–196.

Varela, F., et al. (1992). *The embodied mind*. Cambridge: MIT Press.

Von Hippel, E. (2005). *Democratizing innovation*. Cambridge, MA: MIT Press.

Vygotsky, L. (1929). The problem of the cultural development of the child II. *Journal of Genetic Psychology, 36*, 415–432.

Vygotsky, L. (1962). *Thought and language*. Cambridge, MA: MIT Press.

Vygotsky, L. (1978). *Mind in society*. Cambridge, MA: Harvard University Press.

Wenger, E. (1998). *Communities of practice*. Cambridge, MA: Cambridge University Press.

Wheatley, M. (1998). What is our work? In *Insights on leadership: Service, stewardship, spirit, and servant leadership*. New York: John Wiley and Sons.

White, S. (1989). Foreword. In D. Newman, P. Griffin, & M. Cole (Eds.), *The construction zone: Working for cognitive change in school*. Cambridge: Cambridge University Press.

Zuboff, S. (1988). *In the age of the smart machine: The future of work and power*. New York: Basic Books.

Daniel Araya
Department of Educational Policy Studies,
University of Illinois at Urbana-Champaign

RODRIGO G. BRITEZ

3. OER, ACCESS AND FREEDOM?

INTRODUCTION

Open Education Resources (OER) were first recognized by UNESCO (United Nations Educational, Scientific, and Cultural Organization) in 2002 at the Forum on the Impact of Open Courseware for Higher Education in Developing Countries[1]. The participants of the forum proposed the following definition for OER:

> The open provision of educational resources, enabled by information and communication technologies, for consultation, use and adaptation by a community of users for non-commercial purposes (UNESCO, 2002, p. 24)

The participants of this forum saw OER, and in particular open courseware, as a way to improve the access and transfer of knowledge/information for higher education in developing countries.

The interest on OER was linked with the emergence of the MIT OpenCourseWare[2] (OCW) and other initiatives (e.g. Connexions of the Rice University[3] or the OpenKnowledgeInitiative[4]) that began to use the Internet to make available a variety of contents, materials and tools to be used for educational purposes. Precisely, Johnstone (2005) points out that the advent of those projects generated expectations across a variety of actors related to the possibilities for universities in developing countries of reducing the costs of access to resources and educational materials. Yet, the implications of OCW and other education projects developing OER are highly contested, and still enmesh with larger debates over electronic copyright issues and academic freedom[5]. At a time, we are witnessing the slow emergence of a policy framework for a new Global Information Infrastructure (GII).

In this chapter, I will want to argue that the potential promise of OER for universities is partially mediated by the ways in which the governance communications infrastructure is defined. In short, the promises for education of OER are linked with the political definition of the type of access that those resources will provide. To be more precise, I am stating that different notions of access are mediated by the type of values and political rights which become protected, contested and ignored by institutions and actors participating in the regulation of the infrastructure of digital environments. In those instances, a crucial question to ask is: how are transnational spaces of governance of 'Global Communication' are organized?

M.A. Peters and R.G. Britez (eds.), Open Education and Education for Openness, 33–42.

OPEN EDUCATION RESOURCES AND OPENNESS

First, I need to ask: how is openness is been defined for OER? Hylen (2006) points out that OER are a relatively "new" and essentially contested development linked with:

> ... larger trends towards openness in higher education including more well-known and established movements such as Open Source Software (OSS) and Open Access (OA). (Hylen, 2006, p. 1)

It is contested among other things because of the contentious arguments rise in relation to the meaning of openness in those resources. For instances, Joseph Reagle notes that notion of 'open' used in the discussion about content by online communities is:

> ... implicitly invoking many of the FOSS [Free and Open Source Software] project with which we might be familiar – something like Linux or Mozilla (Reagle, ¶14, 2006)

In short, a notion of 'openness' shared by the OA and the OSS movements that point out to the following common objective: to remove some of the barriers of access/participation to source and information. In a larger sense the notion 'open' can be used to describe increasing degrees of access to:

> Source (democracy, intelligence), project, content (community), publishing, information community, innovation, and system (Reagle, ¶15, 2006).

Precisely, Peter Suber (2005) argues that the Internet and digital media technologies allow the reduction of the cost of production and distribution of information, which leads to the reduction of participation costs. But, as he notes, access does not imply universal access. In the same way openness does not imply 'freedom'. In those terms, new technologies of communication do not necessarily mean a production/distribution of information without cost ('gratis'), instead they

> "imply that the production of information must *potentially* also be politically free" (Schiltz, Verschraegen, & Magnolo, 2005, p. 354).

For instances, openness is contentiously related to the access to expertise able to manage 'codes' of information. It implies potential free access, but does not guarantee the possibility of use. In this point, Felix Stalder (2007) offers a nice analogy about open source software and the legal profession. FOSS allows the users to access the code of programs, the writing law, but not everyone has the time, inclination, and expertise to be a lawyer/programmer, because of

> "its complexity, most people do need to rely on professionals who can interpret the general rules in the light of their own unique situation" (Stalder, 2007, p. 22)[6].

Moreover, it is important to note, that the debate about 'openness' is a politically contested debate about how to codify the meaning and values of 'political freedom' for the production and distribution of source and information in digital environments (e.g. Internet). A fundamental factor in the discussion according to Mathias Klang (2005) is the relevance of the debate over the design and building of infrastructures of communication. In short, will those freedoms to be define in terms of commons (e.g. free speech) or property (e.g. intellectual rights)? Therefore, as Klang indicates, a crucial question in the debate is: "who should own the most fundamental elements of our infrastructures?"

I argue that the answer to this question is directly connected with the political struggle over the definition of the types of 'values' implicit in the design adopted for the building and governance of the emerging GII.

INTERNET AS A GLOBAL INFORMATION INFRASTRUCTURE (GII)

Borgman (2000) offers the following definition of the term GII as:

A technical framework of computing technologies, information content, services, and people, all which interact in complex and often unpredictable ways (p. 30)[7].

From a different perspective GII are not 'new', nor merely a means for access to information. Global telecommunications networks have been present for over a century, and have been regulated in the past by effective international regimes, a political framework for international communication, without which certain order in international telecommunications wouldn't be possible[8]. In those terms, 'Information infrastructure' can be understood in both senses as a technical and public policy framework in terms of people and content.

The term international regime was first coined in 1975[9] in the field of international organization as an attempt to describe the increasing and complex set of international arrangements that took place after the Second World War. Krasner offers the following definition of international regimes:

Implicit or explicit principles, norms, rules and decision-making procedures around which actors' expectations converge in a given area of international relations (Krasner, 1983 Op. Cit. Brahm, 2005, ¶ 3).

To understand the importance of the attempts to build regimes in global communication, I should abandon Borgman's assumption that GII is purely a technical framework, necessarily neutral and unpredictable. On the contrary, I am assuming that GII are assembled according to specific technological frameworks. In this case, I am using this term to refer not merely to technologies, but also the way in which the use of those technologies is codify, organized and regulated in particular ways.

Therefore, I am arguing that technologies once inserted in specific institutional frameworks of regulation, and governance, are used to foster specific values and types of communication. It is in this sense that I understand Castells (2001) contention that the politics of the Internet are about the control of communication

RODRIGO G. BRITEZ

networks, where "the Internet is not an instrument of freedom, nor is it the weapon of one-side domination" (Castells, 2001, p. 164).

Castells argues that the original design of the Internet, as a 'socio-technological infrastructure of communication', was characterized by two fundamental aspects.

First, a 'technological architecture of unrestricted computer networking' was designed to make the communication flows 'difficult –albeit not impossible- to control' (Castells, 2001, p. 169).

Second, an institutional framework of normative references that was the result of the historical context and place of its original development: the United States. In other words, it means "that it came under the constitutional protection of free speech enforced by the US courts" (Ibid, p. 169).

Today, to understand the governance of the Internet in terms of the institutional framework of the US is no longer possible. It is in those circumstances that the discussion over a new regime for GII becomes important: what type of global institutional framework will be built to govern the *use* of new technologies of communication?

At this point, it is important to note that his expansions of the Internet resulted not only in the transformation as the 'de facto' GII, but also the reduction of the ability of each country to control the flows of communication and information.

This led the undermining of one of the traditional sources of power of modern nation-states: their capacity to regulate communication infrastructures. Thus, state and non-state institutions were confronted with the fact of having obsolete technical and institutional tools for the censorship, repression and surveillance of information.

Furthermore, it is important to understand that 'control'[10] becomes more difficult for individual states due to the global character of those networks of communication and the weakening of the mechanisms used by institutions to sustain monopolies or oligopolies over the flow and production of information (Benkler, 2006).

More importantly, this phenomenon is occurring in a context in which the "organizational and institutional tools of governance" (Castells, 2005, p. 9) of nation states in many instances are inadequate to responding to the demands of their citizens. This is in part associated with the growing importance of local problems with a global scope, outside the authority of nation states. In those instances, global governance becomes "an increasingly essential component of national and local governance" (Ibid, p. 10).

The basic resolution to the problem of governance by states has followed three basic strategies according to Castells (2005): participation in network – states, the building of networks of international institutions or supranational organizations around a specific global issue, and the decentralizing of state responsibilities towards local governments and NGOs (Ibid, p. 11).

At the same time a parallel development is observed in the 'unholy' alliance formed between states and commerce to create technologies of control and surveillance. In other words, codes in the architecture of software are being built in order to increase the policing capacities of the states while providing a cover of protection to the intellectual property rights for profit making in the "internet based economy" (Castells, 2001).

It is important to note that the Internet does not erase borders, and different nation states, democratic and authoritarian, have been able to enforce different systems of surveillance and information control according to their own institutional frameworks of regulation.

For example, the case of France in the 2000 injunction against Yahoo Inc, ordering to make 'impossible for French users to access sites auctioning race hate memorabilia' (BBC, 2000). It is not very different in nature to the agreements that Yahoo reached with the Chinese government to censure and monitor information.

That been said, those frameworks of regulation, regardless of their purpose, are part of a common pattern of association between business and state, with profound implications to the way in which free speech is regulated, which can be summed up in the following terms:

> [T]o be doing business with China or anywhere in the world we have to comply with local law[11] (Washington Post, 2005).

In order to 'exercise global regulation', states begin to coordinate their policing systems following the first of the strategies that I mention above: 'as a network state'. They begin 'sharing the effort of information-gathering' (Castells, 2001, p. 179) in 'Cyberspace'. While, there is a unite effort by state and commercial companies to start to regulate the spaces of access to global communication,

> ... through the control of Internet service providers [ISP] and by setting special protocols of surveillance layered on top of the Internet for specific networks, control (and punishment) may be exercised ex post facto (Castells, 2001, pp. 178–179).

For example, the recent ban of You Tube Multiplicity and My Space by Indonesia ISPs in order to block the Dutch film "Fitna" (De Wilde, 2008) or the spicy case in Brazil of a court order to ban a Word Press blog to be implemented by the Abranet (the Brazilian Association of Internet Service Providers)[12] can be see as part of more larger trend of attempts to build institutional capacities to regulate the 'appropriate' content of the flows of Internet communication. In those instances, openness and freedom of speech have very different meanings or relevance according to particular institutional frameworks, defined by nation states.

Against the rhetorical hype of the internet as an unhindered instrument allowing individuals to control their own communication, we have as cold reminders, to mention only two: a) the shut down of the dissident bloggers in Burma last year (The Guardian, September 28 2007), and b) the new layers of the complex system of surveillance and censorship that has been establish by the Chinese government, aptly named the "Grand Chinese Firewall". Thus, I am arguing that the values of freedom of speech in the internet, which can be linked to academic freedom, are politically defined in a diversity of institutional settings and circumstances. Also, I am assuming that academic freedom has always been contentiously linked to the way in which free speech as a 'human right' has been historically defined and redefined by states.

Like the 1990 Dar Salam declaration on Academic Freedom and Social responsibility of Academics, it is possible to state that there is a link between the pursuit of the principle of academic freedom at higher education institutions and the struggle for freedom of expression outside academic settings.

GII, GOVERNANCE AND DEVELOPMENT

It is in this point that the cyber infrastructure under construction and the definition of its global policy framework has become a space of contestation that goes beyond discussions about technical infrastructure. In short, is a contested space over the definition of the purposes and political and economic values that this communication infrastructure will spouse. Therefore, information policy and the participation and influence in the building of the new global regime of communication generate an increasing interest of a number of 'public, private and civil – society policy actors' (Cogburn, 2005, p. 54).

It is important to note that the codification of the institutional values, norms, and rules over the content and purpose, of the design of GII is not only taking place in specific nation states, but also through International Institutions. These are the main mediators and intermediaries in the building of a new policy regime in communication. The Internet as GII is a new 'Cyber infrastructure...based fundamentally on global telecommunication networks' (Cogburn, 2005, p. 53) thus the attempt of coordination and regulation in great measure is dependent on international agreements.

For instance, what would happen if there were an international law forbidding Yahoo or Google to monitor user's activities, as in the case of the journalist imprisonment previously mention in this paper. In the same way, what if there is a codification that said that OER can only can be produces by institutional providers, referred to specific contents, and without public financing.

This is important to our discussion of OER for development and global governance for two important reasons. First, those institutions are the main mediators of the distribution of resources and expertise for the building of the GII in developing countries.

For instance, the role of UNESCO[13] has been critical to expanding the knowledge of those projects in developing countries through the generation of discussion forums that have framed OER within a particular discourse of knowledge sharing, knowledge economy and human rights.

Michael Omolewa (2007) explains that UNESCO activities offer a platform for the creation and promotion of a vast array of professional networks, as well as places of information exchange and potential influence on education development for an increasing array of state and non state policy actors. UNESCO acts as a network fostering the emergence of communications networks around specific issues. In these processes, conferences and meetings constitute spaces of consensus formation that define the type of communication of specific communication networks. Among those specific issues are OER.

For example, since 2004, UNESCO has supported the creation of two related communities of interests (COIs) for discuss about the research agenda and priorities related with the policy implications of OER: the UNESCO Community of interest on Free and Open Source Software (FOSS) and the UNESCO Community of interest on Open Education Resources (OER) communities (Geser, 2007, p. 2).

Second, as Cogburn (2005) points out, those institutions operate, through their conferences, as places of coordination and mediation, between different state and non-state stakeholders, allowing the codification of particular development designs through their reports. Those reports are not merely piece of papers, but later serve to inform and justify the way in which the allocation of resources for the building of GII is taking place in developing countries.

For example, the World Bank is the main provider of financial resources for the building of telecommunication infrastructures in Africa. Their priories of their development loans affect and steer the policy agendas of African nations, including the institutional framework for the provision and regulation of the Internet in their territories.

In this context instances such as the World Summit on the Information Society in 2005 are fundamental spaces of discourse and expert knowledge formation over the information society which influences development policies, including the debates related to nature of openness in OER. It is not a coincidence, the interest of civil society policy actors such as the International Library Associations and Institutions (IFLA) in spaces of definition of this regime for the new GII, such as the World Summit on the Information Society (WSIS). As Ajit Pyati (2007) indicates:

> IFLA participated in the conference as a member of the civil society delegation in both the 2003 Geneva and 2005 Tunis phases of the Conference, and it lobbied government representatives to include language that reflects the importance of libraries, museums and archives to a global information and knowledge society .... IFLA successfully made libraries an important part of the information society vision of WSIS (¶ 5).

The problem like Cogburn (2005) indicates is that those international contexts are characterized to a certain extent by the lack of representation and influence of developing countries and their civil society representatives in the final codification of the policy agreements in relation to rather than with the impact that the lobby of corporate and state interests of advance industrial nations have in the final reports. Those interests are embedded in technocratic views of the Internet and the building of an information society.

CONCLUSION

The information society as a multilayered concept, that as Pyati notes, refers to the different aspects of the constitution and organization of societies around the world in relation to the emergence of this GII and networking technologies of communication is reduced to discussion of freedom in terms of intellectual rights, rather than the constitution of global commons in terms of a more broader conception of political, economic and intellectual freedoms. The problem is that the current consensus of organizing this transnational space of governance and the discussion of OER are still discussed around notions of 'deregulation and faith in market-dominated policies of telecommunications development' (Pyati, 2007, ¶29)

Therefore, the final conclusion of the reports mobilizing development policies carried out by international organizations seem mostly to relate to debates on Internet governance in which important discussions over the sustainability and access to OER seem to be driven mostly by economic perspectives. But, the fact is that the promises of OER for universities in developing countries are not merely related to increasing possibilities of access to information, but also the degree to which the access and use of those resources will be politically free for their users and producers: as an extension of the principle of academic freedom.

NOTES

[1] UNESCO organized this forum with the William and Flora Hewlett Foundation and the Western Cooperative for Educational Telecommunications (WCET).

[2] http://ocw.mit.edu/OcwWeb/web/home/home/index.htm

[3] http://cnx.rice.edu

[4] http://www.okiproject.org

[5] I am using the term following the International Association of Universities (IAU) at the Report on The Feasibility and Desirability of an International Instrument on Academic Freedom and University Autonomy(1998) as the principle that requires " the freedom for the members of the academic community – that is, teaching personnel, students and scholars – to follow their own scholarly enquiries and are thereby not dependent on political, philosophical or epistemological opinions or beliefs though their own opinions may lead them in this direction." (p. 3)

[6] However, most people in this planet cannot afford a lawyer, a programmer or a doctor in the absence of some kind of public commons.

[7] From this perspective a global information infrastructure is a means for access to information (Borgman, 2000, p. 30).

[8] A simple example can be observed the specific allocation of telephone country codes.

[9] Ruggie, 1975, p. 569

[10] Even the illusion of 'control'

[11] This was the justification use by Yahoo's co-founder, Jerry Yang after Yahoo offered the information of a Chinese journalist, complaining about the attempts to news manipulation in a pro democracy website, to the Chinese government. This later led to a ten year conviction of the journalist.

[12] The case was described by the Brazilian judge in the following terms: "a very silly girl lets her boyfriend film/photograph her shamelessly having sex, she fights with the said boyfriend (who has kept the records), betraying him with another guy. And he, disgusted, publishes the spicy and intimate scenes on YouTube." (Goes, 2008)

[13] The UNESCO as being a central space of international debate in education, at times have influence process of cooperation and definition of policy problems in developing countries through the establishment of those forums.

REFERENCES

BBC. (2000, May 23, Tuesday). *France bans internet Nazi auctions.* Retrieved May 8, 2008, from http://news.bbc.co.uk/2/hi/europe/760782.stm

Benkler, Y. (2006). *The wealth of networks.* New Haven, CT: Yale University Press.

Borgman, C. L. (2000). *From Gutenberg to the global information infrastructure: Access to 344.* MIT Press.

Brahm, E. (2005, September 1). International regimes. In G. Burgess & H. Burgess (Eds.), *Beyond intractability.* , Boulder, CO: Conflict Research Consortium, University of Colorado. Retrieved from http://www.beyondintractability.org/essay/international_regimes/

Castells, M. (2005). Global governance and global politics. *PS: Political Science & Politics, 38*(01), 9–16.

Castells, M. (2001). The internet galaxy. In *Chap. 6: The politics of Internet II: Privacy and liberty in cyberspace* (pp. 168–187). Oxford. Oxfordshire: Oxford University Press.

Cogburn, D. L. (2005, Summer). Partners or pawns? Developing countries and regime change in global information policy governance. *Knowledge, Technology, & Policy, 18*(2), 52–81.

De Wilde, G. (2008, April 4). Indonesia lifts ban on YouTube. *Daily Telegraph.* Retrieved April 8, 2008, from http://www.telegraph.co.uk/arts/main.jhtml?xml=/arts/2008/04/11/bbindonesia111.xml

Geser, G. (2007). Open educational practices and resources: OLCOS Roadmap 2012. *Open Learning Content Observatory Services.* Salzburg, Austria.

Goes. (2008, April). *Brazil: Bloggers united against Wordpress ban.* Global voices online. Retrieved April 8, 2008, from http://advocacy.globalvoicesonline.org/2008/04/12/brazil-bloggers-united-against-wordpress-ban/#more-254

Hylén, J. (2006). *Open educational resources: Opportunities and challenges.* Retrieved April 25, 2005, from http://www. oecd. org/dataoecd/5/47/37351085. pdf, Stand, 17, 2007.

International Association of Universities (IAU). (1998). *Report on the feasibility and desirability of an international instrument on academic freedom and university autonomy.*

Johnstone, S. M. (2005). Open educational resources serve the world. *EDUCAUSE Quarterly, 28*(3), 15–18.

Krasner, S. D. (1983). Structural causes and regime consequences: Regimes as intervening variables. In S. D. Krasner (Ed.), *International regimes.* Ithaca, NY: Cornell University Press.

Klang, M. (2005, March). Free software and open source: The freedom debate and its consequences. *Firs Monday, 10*(3). Retrieved April 8, 2008, from http://www.firstmonday.org/issues/issue10_3/klang/

Omolewa, M. (2007). UNESCO as a network. *Paedagogica Historica, 43*(2), 211–221.

Pyati, A. (2007, October). A critical theory of open access: Libraries and electronic publishing. *Firs Monday, 12*(10). Retrieved April 8, 2008, from http://www.uic.edu/htbin/cgiwrap/bin/ojs/index.php/fm/article/view/1970/1845

Reagle, J. (2006). Notions of openness. In *FM10 openness: Code, science, and content: Selected papers from the first monday conference* (Vol. 11). Retrieved April 15, 2007, from http://numenor.lib.uic.edu/fmconference/viewabstract.php?id=36 http://reagle.org/joseph/2006/02/fm10-openness.html

Ruggie, J. G. (1975). International responses to technology: Concepts and trends. *International Organization, 29*(3), 557–583.

Schiltz, M., Verschraegen, G., & Magnolo, S. (2005). Open access to knowledge in world society. *Soziale Systeme, 11*(2), 346–369.

Stalder, F. (2007). *Open cultures and the nature of networks.* City: Ram Distribution.

Suber, P. (2005). *Open access overview: Focusing on open access to peer-reviewed research articles and their preprints*. Retrieved April 25, 2005, from www.earlham.edu/□peters/fos/overview.htm (2005, September 18, Sunday). Obeying orders. *Washington Post*, p. B06. Retrieved from http://www.washingtonpost.com/wpdyn/content/article/2005/09/17/AR2005091701135.html

UNESCO. (2002). *Forum on the impact of open courseware for higher education in developing countries*. UNESCO, Paris, 1–3 July 2002: Final report.

Rodrigo G. Britez
Department of Educational Policy Studies,
University of Illinois Urbana-Champaign

SHIVALI TUKDEO

4. THE POWER OF P2P

Information Networks, Social Organizing and Educational Futures

INTRODUCTION

The rise of networked information environments has enabled a change in thinking about information production, social allegiance and political participation. At the same time, a range of technological innovations have, in turn, brought changes to these very information environments, creating opportunities for loose and tight collaborations among individuals as well as groups. The remarkable possibility of generation, exchange and mutation of information has shaped the areas as distinct as online businesses, open courseware, citizen journalism and social networking to name a few. In comparison with the tenets of social platforms that were available in industrial economy of the twentieth century, the emergence of networked information economy has opened up practical dimensions to political participation (Chadwick, 2006; Hill & Hughes, 1998). Yochai Benkler's work (2006:3) *'The wealth of networks: How Social production transforms markets and freedoms'* begins by recognizing two parallel moves in the economically advanced societies that have made it possible, to a certain extent, to reduce the hold of market-based production.

The first move, in the making for more than a century, is to an economy centered on information (financial services, accounting, software, science) and cultural (films, music) production, and the manipulation of symbols (from making sneakers to branding them and manufacturing the cultural significance of the Swoosh). The second is the move to a communications environment built on cheap processors with high computation capabilities, interconnected in a pervasive network—the phenomenon we associate with the Internet. It is this second shift that allows for an increasing role for nonmarket production in the information and cultural production sector, organized in a radically more decentralized pattern than was true of this sector in the twentieth century. The first shift means that these new patterns of production—nonmarket and radically decentralized— will emerge, if permitted, at the core, rather than the periphery of the most advanced economies. It promises to enable social production and exchange to play a much larger role, alongside property- and marketbased production, than they ever have in modern democracies.

M.A. Peters and R.G. Britez (eds.), Open Education and Education for Openness, 43–55.
© *2008 Sense Publishers. All rights reserved.*

Benkler is not alone in pointing out that the decentralized character of networked information economy has facilitated cooperative mechanisms that do not depend on proprietary logics (van Dijk, 2005; Castells, 1997; Kolbitsch and Maurer, 2006). The move away from proprietary systems also signals a shift from corporate, mass mediated public sphere to that of the networked public sphere, and from mass-media markets to those with more possibilities for individual contribution. Non-commercial and volunteer produced information has called into question the age old skepticism about the quality and viability of volunteer production.

> There are no noncommercial automobile manufacturers. There are no volunteer steel foundries. You would never choose to have your primary source of bread depend on voluntary contributions from others... Widespread cooperative networks of volunteers write the software and standards that run most of the Internet and enable what we do with it...What is it about information that explains this difference? Why do we rely almost exclusively on markets and commercial firms to produce cars, steel, and wheat, but much less so for the most critical information our advanced societies depend on? Is this a historical contingency, or is there something about information as an object of production that makes nonmarket production attractive? (p. 35)

Relatively unknown and secluded at one point, the Internet and its applications underwent significant changes since 1970s. Three autonomous processes contributed to the shift: the economy centered on globalized capital, flexibility and fast pace; the development of computing and communication technologies; and a renewed emphasis on transparency, accountability, individual freedom and connectivity in social life. The astonishing rise of the Internet is historically produced by coming together of several unusual forces including military research, corporations, big science and emancipatory subcultures. While the Internet was a continuation of age old networks of communication and contact, what set it apart was the possibility of "communication of many to many, in chosen time, on a global scale" (Castells, 2001). Another remarkable point about the Internet was that, by using it the users were able to change its nature and scope. The collective communication operative made it possible to transcend the institutional and state controls on information.

This chapter looks at information networks within the contexts that produce them and their connection to other networks. Internet, in its most basic form has connected individuals to information. This chapter focuses on how the Internet is practiced and perceived as a medium of communication. Specifically, I look at the instances of media blackout in Indonesia and Pakistan that resulted in the creation of horizontal production of information, that called into question government regulations as well as the production and consumption of corporate media. Taking the thread further, the chapter looks at Open Education and the practices of producing and sharing information outside of institutional structures.

THE HISTORY OF INTERNET

The short history of the Internet can be traced back to the 1950s when the US department of defense established Advanced Research Project Agency (ARPA). In the wake of cold war, ARPA brought together representatives from universities and corporations to launch ARPANET. Associated with ARPANET was the Information Processing Techniques Office (IPTO) that was developed in collaboration with Rand Corporation and the British National Physical Laboratory. In the subsequent stages, ARPANET was connected to other computer networks and soon it was transferred to the Defense Communication Agency (DCA). The past 50 years of research and development of the Internet was undertaken by numerous academic institutions, corporate research labs and defense units. Len kleinrock's paper 'Communication Nets' (1962) and Paul Baran's work "On Distributed Communications Networks" (1964) were the highlights of 1960s. The first basic email program was written in 1972 at ARPA and Intel corporation released the 8080 processor in 1974. With IBM's first PC in 1981and design of Domain Name System (DNS) in 1983 the number of hosts on ARPANET grew[1] By 1990 ARPANET was decommissioned for not being technologically apt. It was during this time that a number of Internet service providers built their own networks and began setting up their gateways on commercial basis. The ARPANET design including a multilayered, decentralized architecture and open communication protocols was employed by the service providers. In October 1994 the first commercial browser Netscape Navigator was released. Surpassing over a billion users in the year 2005, the Internet usage has grown meteorically since 1995 when there were 42 million users[2]. However, the growing numbers of internet users do not indicate the overarching activities organized around internet. Internet-based networks now occupy an important place in the structuring of core economic, cultural and social actions around the globe. One of the biggest strengths of the Internet was its open architecture, which promised self-evolution. In fact, various components of openness including the decentralized and multidirectional architecture, open communication protocols, and susceptibility of modification were significant in the massive growth of the Internet. The fact that the Internet engaged with, and eventually transformed the social practice of communication is another reason for its widespread reach. Online communication facilitated new patterns of social interaction that were no longer dependent on locality. A peculiar kind of sociability came to be formed through the Internet that was able to de-emphasize the role of physical sites as sole generators of social interaction and community building. Instead, online communication expanded the range of weak ties such as communities of interest and numerous short-term and long-term networks built around emotional support, enjoyment and civic involvement. The structure of weak ties is such that people can join and leave the community as they wish and they are not required to disclose their true identity. The ever growing networks built on common interests, ideas, and information indicate the strength of weak ties. Simply put, the Internet with its wide reach, horizontal architecture and relative cost-effectiveness can be seen as an ideal means to disseminate information, enhance participation and thus help create a democratic social realm (Ferdinand, 2000; Wilhelm, 2000). The actual relationship between the Internet, information production and democratization is much complex and is emblematic of the emergence of information-centric economic and social activities. In fact, information exclusion is one of the most injurious forms of exclusion in the economic and cultural arrangements of advanced capitalist countries. In this perspective, the Internet is instrumental in expanding the reach of information that was previously confined to the power elite. The following three assumptions are at work, shaping the ways in which the Internet is linked to democratization of information and enhanced participation. First, information is increasingly being understood as an essential component of citizenship formation. The influence of information is directly visible in the areas of governance where policy decisions reflect the judgment of the demos. Second, the Internet allows for dialogic and deliberative practices among participants. Such facilitation involving interactive circuits of many-to-many is useful to a create substantive engagement. Third, the Internet provides unmediated communication and decreases reliance on both, the elected officials and interest groups, thereby altering the nature of traditional political intermediaries that involved expert groups, news media conglomerates, government organizations and similar culturally elite groups (Castells, 2001).

RESISTANCE POLITICS IN INDONESIA

The recent political history of Indonesia is fraught with contestations revolving around the challenge of nation-building in the postcolonial context. Nationalist orientation became a project of foremost importance in independent Indonesia where the New Order regime of President Suharto (1966-1998) sought to centralize the control of communication and information services. Established in 1962, the Television of the Republic of Indonesia (TRI) was a state-operated media that actively took part in creating a distinct national cultural space in the country. Since television media was operated under the State, getting information from alternative sources was virtually impossible. The print media was mostly privately owned, yet it was closely monitored and occasional critiques of the government were met with censorship and termination. Imposition of two bans on *Tempo*, the leading news weekly is a case in point. The publication was banned for two months in 1982 for its reportage on riots during the election campaign. Critical reporting of Suharto's administration cost the second ban that was enforced in 1994 and the weekly resumed in circulation only in 1998 after the removal of Suharto regime[3].

Amidst political turmoil and centralized media control, the Internet made its way to Indonesia in early 1990s, initially confining to a small section of the society. IPTEK-Net, the State's first internet network was developed in 1994 and by 1995 Indonesia had an estimated 15,000 users who accessed the Internet through 5 private service providers. In her narration of the spread of Internet in Indonesia, Lim (2003a) draws attention to the social practices of information accessing. The most significant place to access online information in Indonesia was *Warnet*, the Internet Café. Historically, *Warnet* signified a place for social interaction and informal exchange. Lim's ethnographic account of the Internet in Indonesia recalls the spatial and cultural rearrangement of Warnet in order to provide online services. "A Warung[4] can be physically located in the front part of the house, usually in an earstwhile guestroom. Alternatibely, it can be built as a room extension in the frontyard or on the street. Warung usually consist [sic] of just one small room with one table However, sometimes they have a bigger room allowing for more than one table... A common feature of Warung is the *Krepyak*- a bamboo curtain..." (Lim, 2003a:277)

Warung/Warnet gave its users an opportunity to connect and communicate with others without strict control of the State. The internet cafés were not simply places to access web, but were indicative of the transformation through and by technology. The connectivity enabled through internet had an impact on the local resistance movements against the regime. Early accounts of volunteer-based information exchange involved formation of "Apkabar", a popular mailing list started by transnational Indonesians. Along with information-sharing and connecting with other people, the email listservs and virtual interest groups served as spaces that helped shape the 'resistance identity' online. "What started as a mailing list... became a virtual organization to discuss *warnet*-related issues. However, it developed later into a space for discussion on a wide choice of topics ranging from technical computer-related problems to topics such as the monopoly power of the state-owned company and telecommunications regulations and policies. The list had its own motto: "The association is virtual, the fight is real." (Lim. 2003B:121).

Another significant instance of information exchange involved circulation of a satire entitled "The List of Suharto's Wealth" written in the form of successive emails[5]. The email was picked by numerous Indonesian websites, circulated widely through email networks and modified with newer details and in ways to better suit the readers. Similarly, the online publication of "Indonesia Baru", a series of political critiques was received well. The information networks were not confined solely to the net. The politically salient information available online was printed, photocopied and distributed widely. "The photocopied version of "The List of Suharto's Wealth "was commonly found on the streets during March-May 1998. Newspaper sellers and street vendors sold this photocopied version at traffic lights, gas stations, and bus stops and stations... From here the information reached ordinary people in cars, motorcycles, buses, and other public transport." (Lim, 2003a:282) This information hub contributed to the brewing resistance on the ground that had built a successful momentum against the regime. In the first 3-years of its existence in Indonesia, the potential of Internet was understood by individuals and groups alike engaged in social organizing against the government control on public expression. Particularly, the possibility of accessing international media, availability of information through emails and the listservs and relative anonymity were some of the crucial reasons for deploying internet in organizing[6].

EMERGENCY IN PAKISTAN

On November 3, 2007, General Pervez Musharraf suspended the constitution, removed the Chief Justice and declared martial law or emergency rule in Pakistan. The immediate context of emergency imposition lingered on a possible supreme court judgment that might have prevented Musharraf from contesting elections. The declaration of emergency was quickly followed by a blackout of non-government television channels, inaccessibility of cell phones, arrests of civil rights activists and the presence of paramilitary units surrounding the Supreme Court. The emergency rule was not an anomaly in Pakistan where the executive arm of the military has been quite visible in civic life. Tariq Ali (2007) for instance, called the emergency enforcement in November a ritual antibiotic– "in order to obtain the same results one has to keep doubling the doses." Incidentally, Musharraf had suspended the Chief Justice Iftikar Chaudhry in March 2007 and this led to a series of protests across the country, making the administration reinstate justice Chaudhry in July. On the day of emergency, the Pakistani government introduced amendments to two ordinances placing drastic restrictions on the media. The Newspapers, News Agencies and Book Registrations Ordinance and Pakistan Electronic Media Regulatory Authority (PEMRA) ordinance included the following prescript for the print and electronic media:

> To ensure that no anchor person, moderator or host propagates any opinion or acts in any manner prejudicial to the ideology of Pakistan or sovereignty, integrity or security of Pakistan. To not broadcast anything "which defames or brings into ridicule the Head of the State, or members of the armed forces or executive legislative or judicial organs of the State." To not broadcast any program "inciting violence or hatred or any action prejudial to maintenance of law and order."(The Gazette of Pakistan, 2007)

Numerous bloggers of emergency have noted the shockingly short span of time in which approximately 35 television channels were taken off air and how quickly cell phones became inaccessible. The initial accounts of media restrictions included how a private news- channel was raided by the police in order to confiscate its broadcasting equipment; how the Dubai-based channel, Geo TV was taken off air; and how the ubiquitous FM radio stations had been closed. In the absence of television and radio, the Internet became a source-to-go-to for receiving and updating information. Barely 24-hours in the emergency rule, the first Wikipedia entry entitled "2007 Pakistani State of Emergency" was put up [http://en.wikipedia.org /wiki/2007_Pakistani_state_of_emergency]. An autonomous student blog *Emergency Times* started on November 4 that gave information about organizing efforts on ground, protest schedule and legal rights during emergency. The Facebook group "We Oppose Emergency in Pakistan" drew thousands of members in a short time and began sharing stories, video clips and news about emergency. The Pakistani media responded to the ordinances in different ways. First, the television networks and newspapers turned to the Internet and began live web-streaming on a continuous basis. Secondly, news channels began broadcasting via satellite dishes for those who could afford. While the mainstream television media relied on satellite subscribers and went online to broadcast, the protest participants, bloggers and citizen journalists posted their takes on emergency online. Short Message Service (SMS) was used to connect and share information. Student protesters and their supporters used the web extensively in order to update information and outreach. The very first edition of *Emergency Times* for instance, focused on the meaning of emergency in everyday social life; offered practical pointers to protesters, and called for groups to share their protest schedules and pictures.

The purpose of focusing on information networks and collaborations in the context of different forms of media control in Indonesia and Pakistan is to articulate how information exchange has become an important part of political organizing. To revisit Benkler's question, why do people turn to non-market and non-State-controlled forms of information? The horizontal, many-to-many structure of the Internet enables people to give their input from where they are based and what *they* see. In practice, the simple act of peer-to peer information sharing effectively re-writes the sanitized narrative manufactured by corporate media. While the objectives of online forums are varied and they are accessed by a wide range of users, the practice of online information production, circulation and reception goes beyond the classical understanding of a 'communicative event' constitutive of its three nodes: sender, receiver and communicative intent. In fact, questions focusing on the purpose of the sender and expectations of the receiver do not take us much further in understanding the web of information-communication through internet.

From cute-cat-postings to that of special interests, the web is both tied to the attitudinal variants of its participants and is autonomous of it. Without knowing the receivers or producers, the information is put up; modified, and accessed. The horizontal structure of internet along with its capacity to inform, organize and recruit has led to the medium being increasingly used by social movements. The actual relationship between processes of social/political change, social movements and the role of Internet is complicated. As scholars of new media point out, the place of internet in contemporary social landscape is more than an instrument of communication (Dutton, 2000; Castells, 2000; Schuler & Day, 2004). There are two interrelated points with which this relationship can be understood. First, the dynamics of social movements have aligned well with the relatively open structure of the Internet and benefit from its wide reach and small price. The logic of collective action in the 21st century is increasingly geared towards demanding institutional transformations. Actions for these transformations are organized by ideational and cultural materials. Capturing the connections between internet and contemporary social movements of the network society, Castells (2001:139) states,

> ... To build on a historical analogy, the constitution of labor movement in the industrial era cannot be separated from the industrial factory as an organizational setting (although some historians insist on the equally important role of the pub in this respect)... the internet is not simply a

technology: it is a communication medium and it is a material infrastructure of a given organizational form: the network.

The second point relates to the extent online networks become meaningful to local communities in the larger context of their priorities. Online networks help promote discussions, outreach and seek allies to strengthen local groups. They also help internationalize political actions such as the mobilization against the military rule in Myanmar in October 2007 or demonstrations against the war in Iraq. As such, transnational solidarity, awareness building and varied international pressure on political offices in the form of online petitions, signature and phone campaigns now form part of social organizing. Online presence also highlights a possibility of opinion formation that previously resided solely with the hierarchical mass-media. A diversified media, multiple voices, possibilities of volunteer-produced, noncommercial media offer tangible benefits for social organizing.

OPEN SOURCE/OPEN EDUCATION

While working on the connection between geographical remoteness and educational quality, Sugata Mitra (2001) carried out an experiment 'the hole in the wall' that has since then opened a series of questions about self-organizing systems of learning. The experiment, first in a series, was carried out in Kalkaji, a suburb of New Delhi, India and

> [It]consisted of installing a computer connected to the Internet and embedded into a brick wall near a slum. We observed that most of the slum children were able to use the computer to browse, play games, create documents and paint pictures within a few days.

Mitra observed that the children developed a collaborative practice of teaching each other. The broader context of this work focuses on minimally invasive and self-organizing components of education. Virtually absent in formal structures of schooling, the collaborative self-learning enables learners to actively construct knowledge, integrate new information into their preexisting simple ideas that attain complexity in the process. Mitra makes a forceful argument for using minimally invasive systems to address the gaps left by iniquitous resources available to schools. Of course, in order to design education around self-organizing principles, there needs to be a conceptual overhaul of the individual-centric nature of education and teacher preparation.

An urgent rethinking of current models of education is necessary, especially in the emergent articulation of knowledge economy and the role of education therein. The emergence of knowledge economy is linked to the ongoing transformation of capitalism from "a mass production system where the principal source of value was human labour to a new era of 'innovation-mediated production' where the principal component of value creation, productivity and economic growth is knowledge." (Houghton & Sheehan, 2000). The rise in knowledge-intensive economic activities has influenced the understanding of information, learning and skills whereby a growing instance of codification of information, knowledge and culture has acquired importance. Forging a necessary connection between knowledge and development, universities are considered to be future service industries that will play a major role in the mode of production. Reorienting the economic with information at the core, knowledge economy posits for a convergence of education, research and development, and entrepreneurship. Educational institutions are understood to be the key agents of innovation system as human capital providers and connectors between knowledge and business firms.

Emerging out of the very knowledge-intensive and information-networked domains, the development of open education offers a rethinking of an array of practices. Open education is derived from the Open Source model that has enabled a successful techno-political movement based on creative and cooperative practices. Peer production, sharing and emendation are some of the important elements of open source through which the movement sought to create a new kind of information environment. It is hoped that the creation of non-proprietary, 'open' information environment 'both depends upon and encourages great individual freedom, democratic participation, collaboration and interactivity' (Peters, 2007).

As such the users of Open Source Software can have an access to the source code; use the software according to their wish; augment, modify and improve it and redistribute it to other users. Similar to open source, the concept of openness based on access, sharing and revision in a commons-based production has been extended to a range of areas including open content, open courseware, and open education among others. Wikipedia, one of the most popular open projects is based on distributed expertise, offering tools to anyone with internet access to contribute to knowledge building. Explaining the scope of open education, Toru Liyosh states,

> The main tenet of open education is to make educational assets freely available to the public. This is becoming easier and less expensive as network and multimedia technology evolves. Indeed, tens of thousands of open educational resources already exist online, from well-packaged course materials such as MIT's OpenCourseWare project, which allows anyone with Internet access to browse and use MIT course materials, to educational software such as physics professor and Nobel laureate Carl Wieman and his colleagues' Physics Education Technology project, An initiative like the Sakai Project, for example, which is working to design, build, and deploy a new online education platform that includes course management, electronic portfolio, assessment, collaboration, communication, and other tools actually coordinates multi-institutional collaborative efforts and offers institutions the chance to collectively advance teaching and learning. (The p2p foundation)

Open educational projects continue to grow at a rapid pace with an interesting convergence of teachers, students, technocrats, educational foundations, publishing industry and corporations. The Cape Town Open Education Declaration (2007) puts forth some of the tenets of open educational resources.

> They contribute to making education more accessible, especially where money for learning materials is scarce. They also nourish the kind of

participatory culture of learning, creating, sharing and cooperation that rapidly changing knowledge societies need. However, open education is not limited to just open educational resources. It also draws upon open technologies that facilitate collaborative, flexible learning and the open sharing of teaching practices that empower educators to benefit from the best ideas of their colleagues.

The declaration extends its address beyond educators and students to that of institutions and policy makers by touching upon some of the complex issues in the debate: accreditation, assessment and quality control. The basic tenets of openness–horizontal, nonproprietary networks of production acquire different meanings and relevance depending on the focus and structure of a particular open community. While an open project such as Open Source Food (OSF) has chefs sharing and improving recipes, the initiatives like Open Source Religions are created through a continuous process of refinement and extension by the believers themselves. In comparison to traditional religions – which are considered authoritarian, hierarchical, and change resistant – they emphasize participation, self-determination, decentralization, and evolution. (Wikipedia, 2006).

A glimpse of the diverse and complex terrain of Open Source can be seen in Coleman (1999)

> The meanings, aims, visions, and aspirations of the open source community are difficult to pin down.... closer inspection of the movement reveals a cacophony of voices and political positions: anarchic ideals of freedom, "tribal" gift economy rhetoric, revolution, Star Wars imagery, web manifestos, evangelization to the corporate sector, the downfall of the "Evil Empire" (a.k.a. Microsoft), grassroots revolution, consumer choice and rights, community good, true market competition, DIY (Do it Yourself) culture, science as a public good, hacker cultural acceptance, functional superiority, and anti-Communist rhetoric are but a number of the terms, images.

The Open Source, in its various avatars, has created collaborative online presence and in doing so it has attempted to shake,–albeit less explicitly in some forums than others– the hierarchy-laden structures. The Open Source philosophy, with its emphasis on individual freedom and information-democracy brings to light some of the questions that are pertinent to network society. Who owns information? How is the discursive construction of information commons related to the ideal of commons in its material and cultural forms? What are the ways in which open educational practices affect the institutions of learning, even as these practices are being co-opted by the institutions? These questions lead us to think about the relationship between the open movements working to transform the information environments and the social movements working toward political transformation.

CONCLUSION

The emergence of networked information environments has made it possible to connect, dialogue and sustain ties across national borders. The new communication spaces, albeit owned by big media corporations for the most part, do not govern by national regulations alone; nor are they completely free of them. Communication spaces can be reactionary and transformative; political and self indulgent. Physical sites, particularly cultural and institutional spaces have been historically associated with the creation of ideas, informal networks and public opinion. These places of gathering and social interactivity are also embedded in their local particularities. Networked communities operate without the centrality of physical place and its particularities. Decentralized, multimodal nature of the Internet has redefined the concepts such as identity, nationalism and citizenship, among others. But this has not happened outside of material relations; neither has the Internet emerged as the public sphere initiating rational debates and political engagements. Along with the practices of Open Source and innovative organizing by social movements, the Internet is also a grand spectacle of consumerism, corporatization and the manufacturing of public opinion.

The State's encroachment of civil liberties and its control on information led to social organizing in Pakistan and Indonesia. Online networks in general, and peer-to-peer production, update and circulation of information in particular were the medium deployed by political organizers and those outside of the organizing on ground. First, it allows us to see the ways in which new communication technologies are localized and the extent they can bypass State regulations. Secondly, it allows us to see the strategic positioning and engagements of transnational civil society units such as diasporic networks, NGOs and advocacy groups. The underlying thread of analysis is the recognition that today we are witnessing a new period of organizational politics that is involved in creating dynamic oppositional structures at the grassroots; connecting with transnational circuits through networks, and negotiating with the State.

While eschewing the politics of opposition and institutional confrontation, the Open Source movement has worked to democratize the software landscape. Some of the fundamental differences between the Open Source and Free Software Movement bring to surface their distinct philosophies and articulation of problems. The distinction is captured by Stallman (2002) succinctly.

> For the Open Source movement, the issue of whether software should be open source is a practical question, not an ethical one Open Source movement, non-free software is a suboptimal solution. For the Free Software movement, non-free software is a social problem and free software is the solution.

The practices of Open communities are based on values such as individual freedom, information commons, democracy and transparency. Open Educational Resources and Open Courseware initiatives have made interventions in the uneven realm of the production of educational materials. The groups working on social organizing and those engaged in Open communities may have different articulations about the power of institutions, the risk of being co-opted by institutions, and the boundaries of networks. Their practices are, however, largely alike, based on collaboration and free access.

NOTES

[1] A timeline of the development of the Internet can be found here: http://www.webopedia.com/quick_ref/timeline.asp

[2] Statistics of Internet users can be found here: http://www.c-i-a.com/pr0106.htm and http://en.wikipedia.org/wiki/List_of_countries_by_number_of_Internet_users

[3] http://www.amnesty.org/en/library/asset/ASA21/044/2003/en/dom-ASA210442003en.html

[4] Warnet is abbreviation of the word Warung.(Lim, 2003a).

[5] The original email was composed by Aditijondro, an Indonesian professor from Australia.

[6] The influence of mass mobilizations led to the direct actions such as the march in Jakarta; followed by the occupation of the parliament, ultimately forcing Suharto to resign from office.

REFERENCES:

Ali, T. (2007, November 4). Pakistan takes yet another step into the dark night. *The Independent.* Retrieved from http://www.independent.co.uk/opinion/commentators/tariq-ali-pakistan-takes-yet-another-step-into-the-dark-night-398894.html

Bretthauer, D. (2002, March). Open source software: A history. *Information Technology and Libraries, 21*(1). Retrieved from http://www.ala.org/ala/lita/litapublications/ital/2101bretthauer.htm

Benkler, Y. (2006). *The wealth of networks: How social production transforms markets and freedom.* Retrieved August 30, 2008, from http://www.benkler.org

Cape Town Open Education Declaration. (2007, September 14). *Unlocking the promise of open educational resources.* Retrieved August 31, 2008, http://www.capetowndeclaration.org/read-the-declaration

Castells, M. (2000). *The rise of the network society.* Malden, MA: Blackwell Publishers.

_____ (2001). *The Internet galaxy: Reflections on the Internet, business and society.* New York: Oxford University Press.

Chadwick, A. (2006). *Internet politics: States, citizens and new communication technologies.* New York: Oxford University Press.

Coleman, G. E. (1999). *The politics of survival and prestige: Hacker identity and the global production of an operating system.* Retrieved July 14, 2001, from http://www.healthhacker.com/biella/masterslongversion.html

Dutton, W. (2000). *Society on the line: Information Politics in the digital age.* Oxford: OUP.

Feller, J., & Fitzgerald, B. (2002). *Understanding open source software development.* UK: Addison-Wesley.

Ferdinand, P. (2000). *The Internet, democracy and democratization.* London: Frank Cass Publishers.

Fitzgerald, B. (2006). The transformation of open source software. *MIS Quarterly, 30*(3), 587–598.

Hill, K. A., & Hughes, J. E. (1998). *Cyberpolitics: Citizen activism in the age of the Internet.* Lanham: Rowan and Littlefield.

Houghton, J., & Sheehan, P. (2000). *A primer on the knowledge economy.* Melbourne: Centre for Strategic Economic Studies.

Kolbitsch, J., & Maurer, H. (2005). The transformation of the web: How emerging communities shape the information we consume. *Journal of Universal Computer Science, 12*(4), 187–213.

Lim, M. (2003). The Internet, social network and reform in Indonesia. In N. Couldry & J. Curran (Eds.), *Contesting media power: Alternative media in a networked world* (pp. 273–288). Lanham, MD: Rowan & Littlefield.

_____ (2003). From real to virtual and (back again): Civil Society, public sphere and the Internet in Indonesia. In K. C. Ho, R. Kluver, K. C. Yang (Eds.), *asia.com: Asia Encounters the Internet.* New York: Routledge.

Mitra, S. (2001). Children and the Internet. Experiments with minimally invasive education in India. *British Journal of Educational Technology, 32*(2), 221–232.

Open source religion. (n.d.). Retrieved September 1, 2008, from wiki: http://en.wikipedia.org/wiki/Open_source_religion

Peters, M. A. (2007). Opening the book. *The Fifth International Conference on the Book Madrid. Plenary Session Address.*

Schuler, D., & Day, P. (Eds.). (2004). *Shaping the network society: The new role of civil society in cyberspace.* Cambridge: MIT Press.

Stallman, R. (2002). *Why "Free Software" is better than "Open Source".* Retrieved August 31, 2008, from http://www.gnu.org/philosophy/free-software-for-freedom.html

The Foundation for P2P Alternatives. (n.d.). Retrieved August 30, 2008, from http://www.p2pfoundation.net/The_Foundation_for_P2P_Alternatives

The Gazette of Pakistan. (2007). *Acts, ordinances, president's orders and regulations.* Islamabad: Ministry of Law Justice and Human Rights.

Valintino Couros, A. (2004). The open source movement: Implications for education. *Comprehensive Essays.* Retrieved from http://www.educationaltechnology.ca/couros/publication_files/unpublishedpapers/Couros-OpenSource-Comprehensives-June30-04.pdf

Van Dijk, J. (2005). *The network society: Social aspects of new media.* London: Sage Publications.

Wilhelm, A. G. (2000). *Democracy in the digital age: Challenges to political life in cyberspace.* New York: Routledge.[6]

Shivali Tukdeo
University of Illinois at Urbana-Champaign

NATIONAL AND REGIONAL IMPLICATIONS

WILLIAMS MONTEPEQUE

5. OPEN SOURCE IN LATIN AMERICA

Challenges and opportunities for Latin America

INTRODUCTION

Latin America is always behind in any technological movement. One of the reasons is the financial situation of these developing countries in the area. The economies in Latin America are in a real crisis and they do not offer sometimes the most basic and human services to their populations such as education, health, and security. For technological infrastructures, some countries are acquiring certain technologies very slowly, but others are connecting to the Internet at a faster pace. For the Open Access, Open Source, and Open Education movements many barriers exist beyond the infrastructure.

Language, for instance is a factor that affects and limits Open Source to a certain extent. English is the primary language that software developers use to create manuals and documents that contains the source code; possibly translated into different languages later. According to some estimates approximately 80% of the total content of the Internet is in English and approximately 380 million English speakers (English as first language speakers) use the Internet (Miniwatts-Marketing-Group, 2007). But there is a bright future for Latin America because 9% of all the users of the Internet or 113 million users are Latino, that is 25% of the total Spanish[1] speaking population in the world (Miniwatts-Marketing-Group, 2007).

However, that figure includes Latino users in the United States and Spain and those are developed countries. In the US there are 45.5 million Latinos (U.S. Census Bureau, 2008), and 41 million in Spain (CIA World FactBook, 2008), that means that the actual number of people in developing Latin American countries using the Internet is lower than 113 million (80 million users approximately). It's important to know this, because Latinos in the US and Latinos in Spain have more access to technology due to the fact that they live in developed countries. Another statistic that gives hope to Latin America is the growing percentage of users. Between 2000 and 2007 the percentage of Spanish speaking users grew by 360% (Miniwatts-Marketing-Group, 2007). Those are great news for Open Source, Open Access, and Open Education in Latin America.

OPEN SOURCE AND TECHNOLOGY INFRAESTRUCTURE

There is a lot of potential for these movements, and a lot of opportunities for the people of Latin America, but it will be important that governments and institutions

M.A. Peters and R.G. Britez (eds.), Open Education and Education for Openness, 59–67.

make the right decisions to help develop and expand the use and access of necessary technologies to give Internet access to people and the benefits of the global communications and media.

Table 1: Latin American Internet usage
Source: Internetworldstats.com (Miniwatts Marketing Group, 2007)

LATIN AMERICA COUNTRIES/ REGIONS	Population (Est. 2007)	Internet Users, Latest Data	%Population (Penetration)	%Users in Table	Use Growth (2000-2007)
Argentina	40,301,927	16,000,000	39.7 %	13 %	540.0 %
Bolivia	9,119,152	580,000	6.4 %	0.5 %	383.3 %
Brazil [2]	190,010,647	42,600,000	22.4 %	34.7%	752.0 %
Chile	16,284,741	7,035,000	43.2 %	5.7 %	300.3 %
Colombia	44,379,598	10,097,000	22.8 %	8.2 %	1,050.0 %
Costa Rica	4,133,884	1,214,400	29.4 %	1.0 %	385.8 %
Cuba	11,394,043	240,000	2.1 %	0.2 %	300.0 %
Dominican Republic	9,365,818	2,100,000	22.4 %	1.7 %	3,718.2 %
Ecuador	13,755,680	1,549,000	11.3 %	1.3 %	760.6 %
El Salvador	6,948,073	700,000	10.1 %	0.6%	1,650.0 %
Guatemala	12,728,111	1,320,000	10.4 %	1.1%	1,930.8 %
Honduras	7,483,763	344,100	4.6 %	0.3%	760.3 %
Mexico	108,700,891	23,700,000	21.8 %	19.3%	773.8 %
Nicaragua	5,675,356	155,000	2.7 %	0.1%	210.0 %
Panama	3,242,173	264,316	8.2 %	0.2%	487.4 %
Paraguay	6,669,086	260,000	3.9 %	0.2%	1,200.0 %
Peru	28,674,757	7,324,300	25.5 %	6.0%	193.0 %
Puerto Rico [3]	3,944,259	915,600	23.2 %	0.7%	357.8 %
Uruguay	3,460,607	1,100,000	31.8 %	0.9%	197.3 %
Venezuela	26,023,528	5,297,798	20.4 %	4.3%	457.7 %
TOTAL	552,296,094	122,796,514	22.2 %	100 %	590.1 %

Perhaps the biggest challenge in Latin America is infrastructure for digital technologies. Developing countries have limited financial resources, and therefore they do not invest the necessary funding or it's very limited. Also there is a big difference between rural and urban cities or towns in Latin America and developing countries. Urban cities have more access to technology and the new technologies are always implemented and expanded in urban areas first (Atkins, Seely, & Hammond, 2007). Rural areas are almost forgotten and many if not most of them lack electricity and other basic infrastructure.

Before considering the impact and development of the Open Source movement it's necessary to take a look at the current technology infrastructure, Internet access, and users to give an account of the opportunities and challenges for Open Source. Table 1 below provides a good example of the connectivity in the region. The table has the following figures: population in Latin America, number of Internet users, the percentage of penetration in each country, percentage of users per country, and the percentage of growth from 2000 to 2007. This data is important to understand the potential of Open Source in the region.

There is a lot of potential for Open Source because there are approximately 122 million users in Latin America (including Brazil whose official language is Portuguese). And the future is even brighter as more and more people are getting access to the Internet. Some countries are ahead of others as far as connectivity; however countries like Cuba[4], El Salvador, Bolivia, Nicaragua, Honduras, Panama, and Paraguay have less than a million Internet users. These countries need to work hard to create more infrastructures to give more access to people. Even in countries like Brazil, Mexico, Argentina, and Colombia that have a higher number of users, when compared to the total population the numbers are low. In Brazil 22.4% of the population are connected, in Mexico 21.8%, in Argentina 39.7%, and in Colombia 22.8%. However, when looking at the use growth from 2000 to 2007 the percentages are high in most countries. The Dominican Republic reports a growth of 3,718%; Guatemala reports 1,930.8%, and El Salvador 1,650%. Certainly more is needed but the growth of ICTs and the technological infrastructure is growing rapidly in the region.

OPEN SOURCE MOVEMENT IN LATIN AMERICA

Many questions are raised in regards to the Open Source movement in Latin America. One question is: how are users in Latin American going to contribute to the development and creation of Open Source programs? And another question is: are users in Latin America going to switch from licensed software to Open Source software? To answer the first question it's important to keep in mind that English is the primary language that developers generally use to create Open Source software, but the programming source code is a universal computer code.

The impact of people creating or remixing Open Source code and content usually won't take place in Latin America at a large scale, unless there are people that know English and Spanish (and Portuguese) that are willing to contribute to the movement. The major Open Source developments have taken place in the US or developed countries. That is not to say that it cannot happen in Latin America, but there are challenges.

One way to avoid this problem is to facilitate or to allow the "code" documentation to be available in different languages therefore giving the opportunity to developers in Latin America to also contribute to Open Source. This can be done with the publications of many documents in Spanish to allow people to understand how the code works. Before any contribution happens, documents must be translated to help understand the code, and for this task bilingual volunteers are needed.

Searching online I found many websites that invite people to participate in the development of Open Source in different ways in Spanish. Mozilla Firefox for example, provides the opportunity for many developers, programmers, and volunteers that know Spanish to help with translation of documents or developing the new Firefox 2 software.

Developers are encouraged to submit an application for either task if they are interested in helping (Mozilla Firefox , 2008). The other Open Source software or program I checked was the Apache Web Server. Here, I found a webpage in Spanish with information about the software, but the website provided more documents and information about how to use the software rather than collaboration on development for Spanish programmers and translators (Apache.org, 2008). The final website I checked was Linux.org. I searched for Linux in Spanish and I found a website dedicated to the development of the software and to forums in Spanish, (Linux en Español, 2008). The website looks like its counterpart in English. Users are encouraged to participate in collaborate in basic and advanced tasks to develop OS software in Spanish.

It's impossible to look into the different Open Source projects that exist online to see if they have collaboration in Spanish, rather I was looking for the most prominent ones (Mozilla, Apache, and GNU/Linux), to see if they promote OS in Spanish, and based on what I found, I know the future for the OS movement looks bright for Latin America.

The major OS software developers have created websites in Spanish and they invite developers and translators to participate. But despite of all this, I believe that in Latin America people will be more involved in the OS movement as users and promoters, rather than developers and creators of the source code.

This takes me to the second question I proposed above about Latinos switching from copyrighted software and using OS in the region. Latin Americans will most likely be involved in the movement as users and promoters of OS, and will most likely be willing to switch from licensed copyrighted software to OS software for many reasons. One of them is the economical reason; OS software makes more sense in Latin America, because individuals many times cannot afford to pay for copyrighted software.

Also governments in the area have limited financial resources to buy copyrighted software therefore they should switch to OS software. In Latin America economies are in trouble, and people who have access to the Internet, can easily gain access to free software. Checking the Linux.org website I found a list of user groups in different countries. I clicked on a user group from Argentina, and I found 6 communities that meet online, but also that hold live meetings in many places like universities, coffee shops, and hotels. These users believe and support the premise that free is better. They agree completely with the philosophy of the

OS movement and promote it in their respective countries (Linux en Español, 2008).

The Open Source movement in Spanish has different names. I found the following ones online: *Fuente abierta* (open source), *código abierto* (open code), and *software libre* (free software). In Portuguese the movement has the name *"código livre"* (free or open code). Under these names the movement takes place in Latin America and more and more users are joining the movement. Under *"software libre"* I found the website flisol.net or *Festival Latinoaméricano de Instalación de Software Libre*, (Latin American Festival of Free [Open] Software Installation). They have organized festivals or meetings in almost every country in Latin America to receive information about the OS movement, to get free software, and to get help with installation and troubleshooting of OS software and hardware (FLISOL, 2008).

Meetings, conferences, festivals, etc., are taking place in Latin America to promote the OS movement. And many online forums in Spanish exist where people can exchange information, ideas, and programming information. The future for the OS movement looks bright, and the movement will continue to grow exponentially as more people gain access to the Internet. With the growth of infrastructures for digital technologies (including obviously wireless and mobile technologies), more people will become part of the OS movement in Latin America. Some people argue that the FLOSS (Free Libre Open Source Software) movement is growing even faster in Latin America than Asia, and that in countries such as Brazil, Mexico, Argentina, the creation of software is becoming very important.

One of the leading institutions in promoting FLOSS is the University of Texas at Austin. They created the website LANIC (Latin America Network Information Center) to be a network of information regarding Latin America. The website is in English, Spanish, and Portuguese. There is a whole webpage dedicated to free and open software. The information could be browsed by country and they provide information in how to become part of a project in many countries, news about the movement, and general resources (LANIC Free and Open Software, 2008). Another important organization in the movement is the Free Software Foundation Latin America (www.fsfla.org). The website also provides information in English, Spanish, and Portuguese and has direct translations of the philosophy of GNU/Linux and their beliefs about free software (FSF Latin America, 2008).

The leading expert in the OS movement in Latin America is perhaps Cesar Brod from Brazil. Brod has been in contact with Richard Stallman the founder of GNU. Brod wrote a report on the status of the movement in Latin America in 2003. Although most of the statistics in that paper are outdated, Cesar gave an insightful account of OS in Latin America in 2003 (Brod, Free Software in Latin America, 2003). He found out that by searching the term "software libre" in Google per country in 2003, approximately 72,000 pages were found. When I searched the same term (April, 2008), 971,000 pages were found in Spanish in Google when searching only in Spanish. When searching *código livre* only in Portuguese 447,000 pages were found in Google. Brod presented a summary of OS per country, and in 2002, 2003 he did not find any information or did not get any responses from some countries, but in 2008 most countries have networks or communities dedicated to the OS movement.

There are a couple of projects that Latin America has contributed to the OS movement, and those are the GNOME platform, the PHP Nuke project, and KDE standard tools (Noronha, 2003). The countries leading the way in the OS movement are Brazil, Mexico, Argentina, Venezuela, and Cuba. In Mexico, the developer Miguel de Icaza developed the GNOME project, a user friendly desktop that is used in the GNU/Linux operation system. De Icaza founded an open source support and services company located in Boston MA. GNOME is also located in Boston (Brod, Free Software in Latin America, 2003). Red Escolar Libre (Free School Network) is another exciting project from the Universidad Autónoma de Mexico (UNAM). The project was supposed to connect the more than 120,000 public schools in Mexico to the Internet, providing a network server and six desktop computers per school. The Mexican government decided to buy proprietary software from Microsoft for the project instead of using OS software. De Icaza and others are (were) trying to persuade the Mexican government that the same goal could be achieved by using OS software, but the Mexican government has a partnership with Microsoft to complete the project. The ambitious goal was to connect the whole nation online by 2006 (Brod, Free Software in Latin America, 2003).

Brazil the biggest economy in Latin America and with more people connected online (approximately 42.6 million) is the best example for the OS movement. Brazil hosts annually the International Free Software Forums, the biggest IT show in Latin America. Brazil has its own version of a Sourceforge like web portal, called *Código Livre* (www.codigolivre.com.br) and was initiated by UNIVATES (www.univates.br) a small university located in the South of the Country. Brazil also following the Mexican model of free school network developed its own project called *Rede Scolar Livre*. Unlike Mexico the whole project is based on free software, and also provides tools for distance education, computer learning, and network administration. The Brazilian government reported savings of more than $20 million dollars by using free open source software in the project (Brod, Free Software in Latin America, 2003). Argentina is perhaps the country where the movement is more organized. The most important project there is UTUTO, a CD – ROM distribution of the GNU/Linux system that doesn't require installation. UTUTO was developed by Diego Saravia, the engineer that introduced the Linux system to Argentina in 1994 (Brod, Free Software in Latin America, 2003).

The final example of OS and of one the most important ones is found in Venezuela. The developer Francisco Burzi created a web portal, content management system called PHP Nuke to give websites a professional look. From 2000 and on more and more people are using this tool around the world (Brod, Free Software in Latin America, 2003). Brod also has his own Open Source projects. In his website Brod Tecnologia (www.brod.com.br) he has links to the most important OS projects and websites in Brazil. He has formed a partnership with Microsoft to promote discussions and the production of information about the interoperability between OS and proprietary software, allowing users to take advantage of the best of both worlds (www.codeplex.com/NDOS). Other projects for the Linux system include *Navegue protegido* (www.navegueprotegido.org), a website that gives resources to parents, teachers, and teenagers about safety on the web. Another project is *Solis* (www.solis. coop.br/), a website that links free and open source services for implementation and development in many regions (Brod, Projetos, 2008). More OS projects are being developed in Latin American and it won't be surprising to learn about some of them in the future, and how they will benefit the OS community.

The movement is promising, but there are some challenges and limitations. I discussed above the limitation of the language, but there are other limitations and challenges. Perhaps the biggest challenge is a political one (Välimäki, 2004). Välimäki was hired by the Inter-American Development Bank, an institution that lends 8 billion dollars to Latin America, to write a report on Open Source in the region. For Välimäki, countries in Latin America are missing a great opportunity with OS. He argues that economies in the region are in a state of rehabilitation, and they should pass mandates on OS software. He sees OS as the passport for local software business to grow, and for a new generation of Internet users to cross the digital divide. The argument made is that OS software will save governments millions of dollars and can ease the digital divide. Yet many governments in the region are not capitalizing on the opportunity, rather they continue to use copyrighted software, or are simply not paying attention to the OS movement and how is benefiting others around the world. Välimäki explains that Latin America is a complex region, "extreme poverty and extreme wealth, on the one hand one can find bright computing experts and on the other hand people that never used [or seen] a computer before" (Välimäki, 2004).

There are highly creative developers and in many countries there are Internet café projects called *"telecentros"*. The feeling said Välimäki is "certainly a promising one", but he also feels confused because for him "to understand the situation of Open Source in Latin America one must understand politicians as well. None of the proposed initiatives proposed in Peru, Brazil or elsewhere had any impact on reality" (Välimäki, 2004).

Despite any limitations and challenges that need to be overcome, OS makes perfect sense for developing countries because it will reduce the costs for the governments, corporations and non-profits that are interested in helping to break the digital divide in the region and promote a global digital culture. It's not surprising that the biggest transnational software and hardware corporations like IBM, Dell, HP, Microsoft, etc., are investing in Latin America because they see the potential that the market has in the region for their lucrative purposes. OS can give people in the region choices so they do not have to pay for quality software that is free.

CONCLUSION

OS definitely will make an impact in Latin America and most likely Latin Americans will make an impact on OS. Angélica Ospina of the Pan Americas Institution states that "Open Source software is ripe for use in the development community". "[Open Source is] no longer a marginal activity of computer enthusiasts, but an increasing strong alternative to proprietary software creation, adaptation, and use, Open Source could be a powerful tool to assist development in the region" (Camacho & Zuñiga, 2003). For Välimäki one thing is certain, "[F]or the moment, Latin America might be perceived by some people as a place for samba and soccer. In the long term, those hundreds of millions of people will be an integral part of our global information village" (Välimäki, 2004).

Most of those millions of people connecting in Latin America are young people, and they are already participating in great numbers in many of the social network platforms that exists online. Teenagers are especially attracted to these websites to connect with virtual friends around the world. MySpace for example offers the platform in Spanish under the My Space Latino label (http://latino.myspace.com). Hi5.com another social network platform offers its services in many languages including Spanish. Users of Hi5.com can easily switch from one language to another by simply clicking on a link located on the main profile (www.hi5.com). Facebook also could be used in Spanish by changing the profile settings. Google with its social network platform Orkut is also reaching the Latin American market. In October 2007 Google reported that 12.4 million unique visitors or users had accessed Orkut in that area (Kharif, 2007). There is a young generation of Latin Americans who are using the Internet to socialize, but also some of them are helping the OS movement by promoting and using free software, and most importantly by contributing with developing software and translating documents.

To conclude, despite the tremendous challenges in Latin America due to lack of resources, the number of people connecting to the Internet is growing very rapidly. As of December 2007, approximately 122 million people were using the Internet in Latin America (see table 1). This has given Latin America a remarkable opportunity to take advantage and to expand the OS movement. Some developers have made some key contributions already, but in the future due to the expansion of ICTs in region, more contributions will be made.

It makes sense for economical reasons that governments (and people) switch to OS software because it's free. For the development of educational programs and to minimize the digital divide, governments should be using OS software to save money. In Brazil, the government has already implemented the use of OS software in schools; saving millions of dollars that could be utilized in other programs. Perhaps the biggest challenge to the implementation of OS policies or mandates are politics and politicians in the area that lack vision and fail to see the potential of using technologies that are available for free that could easily promote access to the Internet and media technologies. Latin Americans need to be integrated more to the global economy and to mass media and communications. ICTs, the Internet, and OS offer this opportunity and more should be done in the region to achieve this.

NOTES

[1] Portuguese is not considered on these figures, but it's mentioned on page 64 and 65.
[2] *Brazil was not included on the language statistics shown on page 63 because the official language is Portuguese and the statistic was only about Spanish speakers in the world.*

[3] *Puerto Rico is usually included with North America because it's a commonwealth of the US; however is part of Latin America because of the language and culture.*

[4] Cuba has low Internet users due to political restrictions to technologies from the government. This changed recently, as the government has allowed people to buy electronics such as computers and cell phones, etc., but there is no Internet access, the government has an intranet and only people in the government have access. (CIA World FactBook, 2008).

REFERENCES

Apache.org. (2008). Retrieved April 19, 2008, from Apache.org: http://httpd.apache.org/docs/2.0/es/

Atkins, D. E., Seely, J., & Hammond, A. L. (2007). *A review of the Open Educational Resources (OER) movement: Achievements, challenges, and new opportunities.* San Francisco: Williams and Flora Hewlett Foundation.

Brod, C. (2003). *Free software in Latin America.*

Brod, C. (2008). *Projetos.* Retrieved April 21, 2008, from Brod Tecnologia: http://www.brod.com.br/?q=node/189

Camacho, K., & Zuñiga, L. (2003, September). *Open source in Latin America and the Caribbean.* Retrieved April 20, 2008, from The International Development Research Centre: http://www.idrc.ca/wsis/ev-87743-201-1-DO_TOPIC.html

CIA World FactBook. (2008, March 20). Retrieved March 28, 2008, from Spain: https://www.cia.gov/library/publications/the-world-factbook/geos/sp.html

FLISOL. (2008, April 16). Retrieved April 19, 2008, from FLISOL: http://flisol.net/FLISOL2008

FSF Latin America. (2008, April 15). Retrieved April 18, 2008, from FSF Latin America: http://www.fsfla.org/svnwiki/index.es.html

Kharif, O. (2007, October 8). *Google's orkut: A world of ambition.* Retrieved April 20, 2008, from BusinessWeek.com:
http://www.businessweek.com/technology/content/oct2007/tc2007107_530965.htm

LANIC Free and Open Software. (2008). Retrieved April 19, 2008, from LANIC: http://lanic.utexas.edu/la/region/opensource/#argentina

Linux en Español. (2008). Retrieved April 16, 2008, from Linux en Español: http://www.linuxespanol.com/index.php

Miniwatts Marketing Group. (2007, December). Retrieved April 21, 2008, from Internet World Stats: http://www.internetworldstats.com/stats10.htm#spanish

Miniwatts-Marketing-Group. (2007, November). *Internet users by language.* Retrieved March 25, 2008, from Internet World Stats: http://www.internetworldstats.com/stats7.htm

Mozilla Firefox. (2008, January 16). Retrieved April 17, 2008, from Mozilla Developer Center: http://developer.mozilla.org/es/docs/Portada

Noronha, F. (2003, June 2). Retrieved April 17, 2008, from Linux Journal: http://www.linuxjournal.com/article/6915

U.S. Census Bureau. (2008, February 12). Retrieved March 23, 2008, from Hispanic Population of the United States: http://www.census.gov/population/www/socdemo/hispanic/hispanic_pop_presentation.html

Välimäki, M. (2004, April 23). *Latin America's open source: Mañana, maybe.* Retrieved April 20, 2008, from Open Magazine: http://www.open-mag.com/features/Vol_97/OSLA/OSLA.htm

Williams Montepeque
Global Studies in Education,
University of Illinois at Urbana-Champaign

HEIDI A. KNOBLOCH

6. OPEN EDUCATION IN AFRICA:

Challenges and Opportunities

INTRODUCTION

Open Education provides many opportunities and challenges around the world. Of particular interest is the continent of Africa with its vast diversity specifically relating to development. Throughout the Open Systems course, the discussion of Africa, development, and open education was often brought up. No firm conclusions seemed to be drawn while the class mulled old and new thoughts. While it was of meaningful interest to a student in the course because he had been in Ethiopia creating and teaching online courses, it is also of particular interest to me as each discussion brought a trip and a meeting to my mind.

Last summer, I went on a study abroad trip to Pretoria and the area surrounding Pretoria in South Africa. The particular lecture was from a group of people in the University of Pretoria's Educational Technology department. As they explained their quality programs and online courses, they explained that sometimes their work seemed futile as many of their students could not access the courses because of lack of technology. The very students that the country of South Africa needed to access the courses (and more importantly, the degree) were people from the rural community who were without the technological access to what the University of Pretoria offered. This was a meaningful lecture to me because the more we asked questions, the more reality struck me of what had previously been ambiguous terms- digital divide, access, open education. Another realization that occurred at that time was that this was South Africa's prestigious university- what about the rest of South Africa? And the rest of Africa? As I continued to travel into Botswana and then into the volatile country of Zimbabwe- these questions continued. With those faces and places in mind, the following chapter addresses the opportunities and challenges that Open Education has in Africa.

THE STATE OF AFRICA AND THE CHALLENGES TO OPEN EDUCATION

Before a description of Open Education is written, it is important to understand the state of Africa, as this will provide a framework of what Open Education opportunities may or may not provide in Africa. Otherwise, it would be easy to be discussing different ideas or concepts of Africa and sadly, even different stereotypes. With Africa's extreme diversity in almost every area it is difficult and yet necessary

M.A. Peters and R.G. Britez (eds.), Open Education and Education for Openness, 69–77.
© *2008 Sense Publishers. All rights reserved.*

to realize the breadth of this polarization. Since the majority of Africa is still considered in poverty, the poor majority will be the focus of the chapter. *This same description of Africa is also the description of the challenges that Open Education faces in Africa.* The following pages describe the key issues to survival in general as well as issues that Open Education faces in mobilizing this continent. Several words can be used in a discussion of effected lives in Africa such as the AIDS epidemic, poverty, debt, food insecurities and water issues- these are the challenges to Open Education and life in Africa at large.

A GENERAL OVERVIEW OF THE AIDS EPIDEMIC IN AFRICA

The 2006 UNAIDS report gives the following statistics of many countries throughout the African continent:

Both HIV prevalence rates and the numbers of people dying from AIDS vary greatly between African countries. In Somalia and Senegal the HIV prevalence is under 1% of the adult population, whereas in South Africa and Zambia around 15-20% of adults are infected with HIV. In four southern African countries, the national adult HIV prevalence rate has risen higher than was thought possible and now exceeds 20%. These countries are Botswana (24.1%), Lesotho (23.2%), Swaziland (33.4%) and Zimbabwe (20.1%). AIDS has less affected West Africa, but the HIV prevalence rates in some countries are creeping up. HIV prevalence is estimated to exceed 5% in Cameroon (5.4%), Côte d'Ivoire (7.1%) and Gabon (7.9%). Until recently the national HIV prevalence rate has remained relatively low in Nigeria, the most populous country in sub-Saharan Africa. The rate has grown slowly from below 2% in 1993 to 3.9% in 2005. But some states in Nigeria are already experiencing HIV infection rates as high as those now found in Cameroon. Already around 2.9 million Nigerians are estimated to be living with HIV. Adult HIV prevalence in East Africa exceeds 6% in Uganda, Kenya and Tanzania.

POVERTY IN AFRICA

An article in the San Francisco Chronicle published in late 2006 provides a critique of some of the World Bank's effectiveness with poverty in Africa. Although written from a critique point of view, I believe it gave a more holistic view of depravity of the situation as it examined several countries throughout 15 years. For example:

Among 25 poor countries (in Africa) probed in detail by the bank's Independent Evaluation Group, only 11 saw reductions in poverty between the mid-1990s and the early 2000s, while the other 14 suffered the same or worse rates over that term. The group said the sample is representative of the global picture.

The article also gave a perspective about the sustainability of this help. It should be also noted that the article mentions how this is while the economy is thriving, but will the outcome and sustainability still be even as hopeful as this in the years to come?

Even sub-Saharan Africa has grown (GNP) by more than 4 percent annually over the past five years...but the evaluation group study found that growth has rarely been sustained, exposing the most vulnerable people – the rural poor – to volatile shifts in their economic fortunes. Only two in five of the countries that borrowed from the World Bank saw per capita incomes rise continuously from 2000 to 2005, the study reported, and only one in five saw increases for the full decade from 1995 to 2005.

Finally, Open Education and all of the technology that it entails is hard to fathom when the numbers are so bleak for those whole live on less than one dollar a day.

Overall, between 1990 and 2002 the percentage of the world's people who subsist on less than one dollar per day declined from 28 percent to 19 percent, according to World Bank research. By the bank's reckoning, 1.1 billion people were subsisting at that level in 2001.

More importantly the Director/General of the Independent Evaluation Group, Vinod Thomas, goes on to say, "The sheer numbers of people living under the $1 a day definition of poverty has been stubbornly high."[11]

THE DEBT DILEMMA

Less publicized than other more easily people focused is the enormous issue of debt that is more policy focused in Africa. It is this debt that is undermining the very infrastructures that is looking at being utilized for Open Education. The countries can rarely even invest in themselves because they are paying other countries old debts. For example, a campaign against this debt said:

Africa's over $200 billion debt burden is the single biggest obstacle to the continent's development... African countries spend almost $14 billion annually on debt service, diverting resources from HIV/AIDS programs, education and other important needs... Sub-Saharan Africa receives $10 billion in aid but loses $14 billion in debt payments per year.

These are rather large number and large statements, but three countries give a closer picture of what is occurring because of the debt dilemma. "In Burundi, elimination of education fees in 2005 allowed an additional 300,000 children to attend school. While more than 80 million Nigerians live on less than $1 per day, in 2005 Nigeria agreed to pay over $12 billion to the Paris Club of creditors in exchange for partial debt cancellation." The final country gives a picture of what could occur for basic necessities if the debt was not as large. "In 2003, Zambia spent twice as much on debt repayments as on health care. But partial debt cancellation allowed the government to grant free basic healthcare to its population in 2006." These basic necessities for life itself give a picture of the probability of priority for Open Education.

FAMINE OR FEAST? FOOD INSECURITIES

All of these issues are interwoven, but the connection can really be seen in the food insecurities whether it is drought and the environment, debt and international aid, poverty and food prices, or AIDS and undernourishment.

In 2006, Barry Mason wrote an article describing the non-profit organization, OxFam's finding about food insecurities in Africa. While I read the article, the images of Somali people in the news two days ago causing an uprising about food prices that have spiked came to my mind. While these statistics and perspectives on this vast issue are two years old, the insecurity is present if not larger today. Mason and OxFam provided a bleak portrayal of the situation:

> ...whilst the average "developing world" figure for under-nourishment is 17 percent, in sub-Saharan Africa the figure is 33 percent. For Central Africa it is 55 percent. On average the number of African food emergencies per year since the mid 1980s has tripled.

Still the report goes on to reveal the number of people affected in <u>under funded</u> countries. "The UN estimates that 16 million people are at immediate risk in ten neglected and under-funded emergencies in Africa, which include the prolonged tragedies of northern Uganda and the Democratic Republic of Congo." In the interconnection of all these issues, the report points out several, but two are specifically what has been examined previously:

> Maize production on communal farms fell by 54 percent between 1992 and 1997, largely because of AIDS-related illness and death...Rural poverty in sub-Saharan Africa is exacerbated by dependence on the export of a small number of agricultural commodities, many of which face volatile and falling world prices. In 2002-2003, a collapse in coffee prices contributed to the Ethiopian food crisis that same year.I

WATER ISSUES

The water issue brings many faces and places to my mind from my South Africa trip, as this is what we studied throughout the course. It was unfathomable to understand the depth of the water issue even in one country that is considered somewhat "developed" and is much more difficult to understand the issue on the African continental scale. The UN provided a framework for this understanding by providing an article by Gumisai Mutume in 2004 which stated that:

> Although the Johannesburg summit set a target of reducing by half the proportion of people without access to safe drinking water and sanitation by 2015, more than 300 million Africans still lack access to safe drinking water and 14 countries on the continent suffer from water scarcity.

Also, on the continental scale, the article goes on to say, "Out of 55 countries in the world with domestic water use below 50 liters per person per day (the minimum requirement set by the World Health Organization), 35 are in Africa." Continuing to read with the understanding of the challenges to Open Education, I read on to give more of face to this issue.

Almost half of all Africans suffer from one of six main water-related diseases…Water bodies in Africa are shrinking. The size of Lake Chad, for example, has fallen from 25,000 square kilometers during the 1960s to less than 3,000 square kilometers today, affecting more than 20 million people.

The water issue is often taken for granted in the developed countries that are developing Open Education, but what impact does it have on Open Education?

THE CHALLENGES OF AFRICA ARE AN OPPORTUNITY FOR OPEN EDUCATION?

As a Special Education teacher, I truly believe that all people can and should be educated and that education provides the means to overcome challenging life situations. I also believe that it is absolutely crucial to understand these challenging life situations for education to occur. Unless there is a deep understand of the issues, those issues become what education seems to work against instead of education being something to work towards while decreasing the effects of these issues.

There is a complete discouragement of what education has to offer those difficult situations. I see this everyday in my own life. I can show up to work with my students who are considered some of the most difficult teens in the state of Illinois and see them as that- difficult teens. Or, I can choose to show up to work with teens that have been through some of the most traumatic experiences that one should not even have to hear about, let alone live through.

When I keep those things in mind, the progress and even lack of progress seem hopeful and promising, but there are many days that there is a lack of hope- on those days, all I see is the trauma, the past, the system, and even the students in general. On those days, there is truly no hope for even education or me. Sadly, those days occur much too often.

As the above bleak picture of Africa was portrayed, it seems that the same holds true for Open Education. The choice is what Open Education faces in either working "against" these challenges or choosing to work "for" education and in turn decreasing those challenges. The semantics seem small, but it is important that Open Education is not something that will wipe out these challenges and that is it sole purpose. Instead Open Education needs to be seen as providing opportunities and access so that it will then provide a means of departure from these challenges. For example, in Mandarin Chinese, the symbol for the word "crisis" is a combination of the symbols for the words "danger" and "opportunity". Whether it is AIDS, poverty, debt, food, or water, it is evident that Africa is in a crisis. Open Education can see Africa as danger within all of its many challenges or as opportunities within all of its many challenges. The following pages highlight different ways that Open Education can provide opportunities.

WHAT IS OPEN EDUCATION? ⁱ

While the definition of 'open' is still being debated, its very essence may continue to be debated throughout time. In order to be able to have a basic understanding before examining its opportunities for Africa, Stephen Downes from National Research Council Canada provides a few thoughts from his article "Models for Sustainable Open Educational Resources". He writes, "...Walker (2005) defines 'open' as "convenient, effective, affordable, and sustainable and available to every learner and teacher worldwide." He goes on to write that "Daniel (2006), furthermore state 'the 4 As: accessible, appropriate, accredited, and affordable.' A critic would note that there is a significant difference between 'affordable' and 'free'." This is particularly the case for Africa. One must ask what is convenient, affordable, sustainable, accessible, and available to "every learner and teacher worldwide"? Could anything with this description of Open Education be considered in existence? In reflecting on the state of Africa as described above, it seems that nothing like this is in existence. There are several key opportunities in order for it to come to fruition.

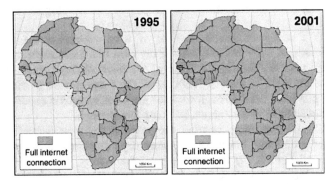

Figure 1. Internet connectivity in Africa¹

Many of the issues in Africa seem to come from a top-down model approach. The solutions may need to be the same specifically in the area of Open Education. Until the policy makers and key players see the importance and potential of Open Education, the people will wait unknowing of what how much more involvement they could have in the knowledge economy than they have in the market economy. In their World Bank report, Michael Potashnik and Joanne Capper (1998) write that "Developing countries now have new opportunities to access knowledge and enhance their human capital." But then they go on to write (this is specifically pertinent to Africa) that "Print is still the cheapest technology, and, even if the costs of using high-tech dissemination tools fall below those of print, it will be some time before many of the countries have adequate infrastructure." Vis Naidoo and Casper Schutte (1999) in their Virtual Institutions on the African Continent begin by writing "For developing countries, the primary emphasis is always upon acquiring infrastructure, such as telecommunication infrastructure, hardware, software, and networks." Soon after, they state, "...All such virtual activities in Africa are limited to the experimentation level or in the initial stages of implementation because of infrastructure problems, which, in turn, are caused by lack of funds and expertise and in some cases political instability." When Naidoo and Schutte wrote the article, Internet connectivity was still a part of what the infrastructure needed to act on, but as seen in the image, Africa is fully connected to the Internet today. While this shows promising potential, there is still a lack of actual connection and technology.

Obviously, Open Education has its basis in technology. Within that, it can be concluded that Open Education has potential in every area of the world, but is only active where adequate technology is. The following statistics given by Dan Eastmond (2000) in his article "Realizing the Promise of Distance Education in Low Technology Countries" provides an understanding as to why he stops calling certain countries "Less Developed" and begins calling them "Low Technology". He writes that:

> DCs (Developed Countries) have 95% of computers... 75% of all phone lines are in 10 DCs; the United States has more than Asia; the Netherlands has more than Africa; Tokyo has as much as all of Africa; and Italy has more than Latin America, In DCs, telephone access is greater than 50%; in African LDCs it is close to 0.3%.

The gap is obviously high. Eastmond goes on to describe four policy changes that would be effective in shrinking the gap that he gets from Prasad 1997. They include:

> (a) access- people in LTCs receive more opportunity to take courses within their nation as well as from abroad; (b) learning from others—distance initiatives can be informed by the previous efforts of others; (c) partnerships—several institutions may combine resources in providing better programs or services than any single one could do separately; and (d) competition- mediocre programs, forced to compete with excellent ones, will improve their quality, efficiency, and performance for survival's sake.

I believe that Eastmond gives an excellent holistic perspective in his conclusion of what it will take. He writes:

> Whether utilizing high or low technology, distance education (can the same be said for Open Education? -My question) can be effective when it fits within the technological infrastructure and cultural context of the LTC. Often, distance education is not a stand-alone solution; rather it fits into structures of classroom education and individual tutoring. As educators in these LTCs gain more experience with all aspects of distance education development, delivery, and evaluation, they will advance suitable models that fit the needs of each country. They will seize opportunities to borrow and adapt suitable models, take calculated risks, and seek economic and political support to discover the appropriate distance education model that meets their country's needs. With continued global cooperation and collaboration with distance education these models can be shared and adapted by others.

CONCLUSION

In Ajaga Nji's chapter titled "Creating a Knowledge Society Through Distance and Open Learning in Cameroon", he examines adult learning. In his conclusion, he very much touches on all of the previous mentioned challenges and opportunities of Open Education in Africa. While he uses the phrase 'distance education', throughout the chapter he uses it interchangeably with 'open education'.

Distance education should not be seen as a panacea for solving the educational needs of a nation in short supply of resources. Rather, it should be seen as a window of opportunity for a nation to maximize the use of limited physical, financial and human resources in its efforts to increase educational access while guaranteeing the quality. In poor nations, distance education is a viable alternative mode of educational delivery for adult learners, farmers, school dropouts and people with special needs and problems. Distance education can reinforce the indigenous knowledge systems of peasants in developing countries, and help governments to remove the barriers to progress that keep poor people poor: the burden and barriers imposed by ignorance, disease, managerial incompetence, and lack of access to new technologies...Distance Education holds Africa's hope as a viable mechanism to build knowledge societies, enhance democracy, encourage good governance, promote citizen participation in public activities, build a culture of civic responsibility and prepare the continent for the formidable challenges of the 21st century.

We must not expect that Open Education can solve all the problems and we cannot expect to solve all the problems before using Open Education. We must fight for what Open Education is- accessible to all. It has great potential in Africa, but the potential must be unleashed.

NOTES

[1] http://web.ges.gla.ac.uk/~mshand/africawww/Image7.jpg

BIBLIOGRAPHY

Downes, S. (2007). Models for sustainable open educational resources. *Interdisciplinary Journal of Knowledge and Learning Objects, 3*.
Eastmond, D. (2000). Realizing the promise of distance education in low technology countries. *Educational Technology Research and Development*, 48(2), 100–111.
Naidoo, V. & Schutte, C. (1999). Virtual institutions on the African continent. *The Development of Virtual Education: A Global Perspective. A Study of Current Trends in the Virtual Delivery of Education*.
Nji, A. (2000). Creating a knowledge society through distance and open learning in Cameroon. In S. Indabawa; A. Oduaran T. Afrik, & S. Walters (Eds.), *The State of Adult and Continuing Education in Africa* (chapter 7). Windhoek: Faculty of Education, University of Namibia.
Potashnik, M., & Capper, J. (1998). *Distance* education: growth and diversity. *Finance & Development*, March, 35(1), 42–46.

http://www.avert.org/aafrica.htm
http://www.commondreams.org/headlines06/1208-06.htm
http://www.africaaction.org/campaign_new/debt.php
http://www.wsws.org/articles/2006/sep2006/hung-s06.shtml
http://www.un.org/ecosocdev/geninfo/afrec/vol18no2/182environ.htm

Heidi A. Knobloch
University of Illinois at Urbana-Champaign

GABRIELA WALKER

7. OPEN EDUCATION AND GLOBAL DIGITAL CONNECT AND DISCONNECT

The Promise of Open Education in Romania

INTRODUCTION

We are on the cusp of a global revolution in teaching and learning. Educators worldwide are developing a vast pool of educational resources on the Internet, open and free for all to use. These educators are creating a world where each and every person on earth can access and contribute to the sum of all human knowledge. They are also planting the seeds of a new pedagogy where educators and learners create, shape and evolve knowledge together, deepening their skills and understanding as they go. (Cape Town Open Education Declaration, 2007)

The concept of Open Educational Resources (OER) was adopted by the UNESCO in 2002 to refer to free access to educational content made available through Information and Communication Technology (ICT) (UNESCO, 2007). Access to educational information and knowledge is made available to any individual with an Internet connection, who can use, adapt, share, create, and re-use it for non-commercial purposes. ICT manipulation assumes a certain level of digital literacy facilitated through the Internet. Digital literacy could be defined as the ability to use digital technology or communication tools and networks to locate, use, evaluate, and produce information. As an evolving concept that mirrors the expanding information needs of our society, digital literacy is an ability emphasized today more than ever before. Digital literacy is one of the skills that enables educational fulfilment (CISCO IBSG, 2007; CISCO, 2008, January). Thus, in the long term, open education impacts employment versatility and competitiveness in an era of globalization.

The Internet, which started as a government-backed military project in 1969 (Hafner & Lyon, 1996; Naughton, 2000; Webopedia, 2006), now has an immense and growing array of uses. Uses of the Internet and the World Wide Web currently include: (1) rapid retrieval of information; (2) dissemination of audio, video, or written information; (3) communication and interconnection; (4) searching capabilities for data and services; (5) distance learning; (6) numerous uses in the classroom; and (7) interdisciplinary resource use (Everett, 2002; Isaacson, 2002).

M.A. Peters and R.G. Britez (eds.), Open Education and Education for Openness, 79–93.

Open education can be delivered in different forms. Examples include programs sponsored by individual institutions (e.g., MIT OpenCourseWare), designs of open software platform to support online learning environments (e.g., Sakai Project), compendiums of open content (e.g., Stanford Encyclopedia of Philosophy, and Wikipedia), and projects that provide instructional tools, such as virtual tutors, simulations, laboratories (e.g., Open Learning Initiative from the Carnegie Mellon University) (Dholakia, King, & Baraniuk, 2006). Thus, open education became a "new" paradigm through which constructivist learner-centered pedagogies, which help learners construct knowledge for themselves. This information is delivered and used complementarily to traditional pedagogies or by themselves, giving birth to a new type of Cartesian learner, the online learner, who is usually separated from the environment. Within the new paradigm, the learner may be physically isolated from other people, but nevertheless able to interact through technology. To complete the image of the online learner, we need to consider the emergent types of learners described, for example (a) by Barab (2001) as the "ecological learner", the knower who is integrated into the context; (b) by Petraglia (1998) as the "Rockwellian learner", one who constructs his or her own knowledge of the world (Sleeman and Rockwell, 1981); or (c) by Beckett and Hager (2002) as the "organic leaner", considered with all his needs, evolving, more social, and interdependent. Nyambe and Shipena (1998) recognized that the new generation learner is a critical global citizen who needs to rise up to the new demands that the emerging global village enforces on the knowledge society.

Aside from making detailed and up-to-date information available to individuals who may be geographically isolated from "brick-and-mortar" libraries, open education provides opportunities for situated cognition, anchored instruction, and multiple ways of learning, models that are emphasized in today's teaching strategies. One of the post-modernist learning theories is the Universal Design for Learning (UDL), which advocates education for all by simply considering the learning and assessment needs of all potential learners or users from the beginning. These types of goal-directed and student-oriented methodologies target both young and advanced learners, since they provide opportunities for users to segment and chunk data from given problems, such as the ability to refer back to specific data segments. For example, it takes longer for a regular videotape to be rapidly played back and reviewed, while most multimedia formats can be readily replayed by users (e.g., quicktime movies). This type of digitally-delivered education can take the form of full-blown multi-media with web pages making use of text, video, audio, and graphics that promote realism, and with possible interactive branching and hyperlinks that promote motivation and understanding. Pisha & Coyne (2001) suggest that ICT tools can "be employed to develop a new generation of flexible curricula and materials that accommodate each student's idiosyncratic pattern of strengths, weaknesses, styles, interests, and background knowledge", emphasizing that the multimedia technologies enable learners to "construct, monitor, demonstrate, and communicate their own learning" (p. 199).

GLOBAL DIGITAL CONNECT AND DISCONNECT

All dimensions of globalization are affected by open access to information, which in turn influences the development of open education through the impact the knowledge has on society, culture, the economy, and politics. Acknowledging the broadness of the concept of globalization and despite the ongoing shifts in its conceptualization, a sociological working definition (Steger, 2003) views globalization as a set of social processes describing humanity's current condition becoming one of globality, that is, globalization is seen as "shifting forms of human contact" (p. 9). As such, open education, made possible by ICTs, provides access to information and knowledge, which in turn enables the opportunity for inter-human communication. According to the computer company CISCO, "communication builds community" (CISCO Systems Inc., 2007, p. 3). Through socialization, the online users accessing open education become a knowledge society. "Cross-cultural exchange can spread greater diversity as well as greater similarity" among the global community (Legrain, 2003, p. B7). However, openness does not mean globalization, but only aspects of it. Appadurai (2007) identifies five cultural dimensions of globalization: (a) ethnoscapes, the variety of individuals and groups in the world; (b) mediascapes, the circulation of information through electronic means; (c) technoscapes, the high- and low-end informational and mechanical technologies; (d) financescapes, the flow of global capital; and (e) ideoscapes, the ideologies of states and counterideologies of various movements. Knowledge enhanced via open education impacts the quality and quantity of all these aspects of globalization, modifying and adapting the principles of governance of all sectors of human activity to the ongoing conditions. Benkler (2003, p. 7), referred to open commons as a space with open access where open education can take place, arguing that "the most important resource we govern as an open commons, without which humanity could not be conceived, is knowledge and culture", including scientific knowledge and academic learning.

The benefits of open education and its positive influences on connecting the global village have been discussed by various authors. For example, Heylighen (2007) mentions that open access to educational content (a) opens opportunities by freely providing software, technical know-how, and scientific knowledge, via suspending the copyright, patenting, or copy protection laws; (b) allows for the production and reproduction of informational content at a fraction of the cost that corporations would have otherwise charged; (c) contributes to the creation and distribution of information more quickly and widely; (d) contributes to social well being through communication, technological efficiency, and economic productivity; (e) enhances the reputation or image of individuals, companies, nations; (f) may bring conventional income (when there is a charge for expertise); (g) provides an example of how the education is produced and distributed (as an indirect benefit); and (h) promotes greater user autonomy.

Through open access, educational information undergoes a cycle of 'use, criticize (provide feedback), and improve' the resource, and in this way innovation takes place. Thus, the producer of the information benefits as much as the user. This is important since innovation is the key to profit and "top ranking" for any corporation. CISCO (2008) for example, admits that their "long-time commitment to ongoing research and development (R&D) is the basis for CISCO's innovation." Economists like Marchand and Horton (1986) talk about information as a corporate resource, systematically managed to provide a cutting edge. However, since only the explicit information is posted while implicit knowledge stays with the producer, the expertise does not change its locus, allowing for potential remuneration gains. By far, the largest benefit of investing in open education is the fact that not only does it create human capital by producing workers in the service of the global knowledge economy, but it can also accomplish it more efficiently (faster and cheaper) and efficaciously (more versatile workers) than traditional education using old-fashioned textbooks. In terms of equity, open education demonstrates gender and color blindness, and eliminates certain biases against physical disabilities, blindness, and hard of hearing population, aiding in the education of the rest of all segments of population with ICT access. In other words, once the "digital divide" is surpassed, you can be who you want to be as long as you can be what you pretend to be.

Some of the challenges of using digitally-delivered education include the fact that open access communities lack the typical control and penalties of social groups, developing according to laws of variation, recombination, and selection, having as exceptions "random fluctuations" or "sequence effects" that may cause a neglect or omission of equally valuable information (Heylighen, 2007). Also, some argue that open educational content is most efficient in the acquisition of higher-order skills and in the synthesis of information rather than in an atomic model of learning, which needs an experiential, hands-on basis, best mediated by human interaction. In addition, there is no strict peer review process to prevent posting of inaccurate or statistically unsound information.

An inherent paradox of open education, as with most forms of media, rests with its character of information decentralization, and, at the same time, centralization. The nature of information is immaterial, multipliable, potentially and partially excludable, but modifiable (by choosing to or not to impose some type of copyright law), and transferable. Thus, by providing global access free of charge and ownership to the educational content, open education contributes to reducing the danger of commercial monopolies that control software standards or information distribution.

However, the sponsors of the open education sources can manipulate the quality and quantity of the content that reaches the audience with access to the World Wide Web, in other words, they can channel selected information to accomplish certain goals. Although the information itself is not commercialized, marketing and advertisement models present everywhere in the media may infiltrate the educational websites, shaping the behavior of the learner, now a consumer, in a way that can be translated into consumption. Also, the flow of information can be traced to the Internet Protocol address, and thus more control can be exerted when needed (e.g., by authorities). Making educational content widely open for access may then take a form of covert manipulation and may gear the use of open education towards or against the globalizing interests. The trends of popular information and knowledge may lead to standardization and normalization with repeated uses, making us forget that data can become obsolete, hence unreliable and uncertain, very quickly. In the age of informational saturation and confusion, meaning-making becomes increasingly difficult because the source of the information is not always stated, and therefore its truthfulness may be questioned. An unconsidered view of the electronically posted information could be misleading, and data can be taken out of context without the employment of evaluative and critical skills. For example, the majority of people remain at the level of information sharing, which means that they employ neither a critical engagement with the piece nor learning, thus creating a good medium for manipulation and deception (Fryer, 2004). In this sense, the Internet can, in the wrong hands, become a tool for propaganda. Thus, the open system may not always foster an analytical understanding of the truth and the reality, but could become merely an entertainment tool or "edutainment" (Peters, 2007), capable of distracting people from the meta-goals of education and real life, thus fulfilling the principle of "sequence effects" mentioned earlier. For example, in 1994, when the genocides in Rwanda and Kosovo were unfolding, the famous O. J. Simpson case was given more media attention most days in Anglophone and developed countries.

Superficially, it looks like open education serves the global society and economy by advancing and circulating knowledge, but with it come downsides stemming both from its mediation through technology and from its other inherent characteristics. Because open education relies on access to multimedia, there is a danger of prioritizing efforts towards acquiring and advancing of technology rather than in the process of education itself. The Information for Development Program (2005) argues that there is a mismatch between achievements measured by standardized tests following the "new" pedagogies and following traditional pedagogies. Hence, ICTs are not only shown not to be central to the process of learning, but, in fact, they can interfere with pedagogy. Taking into consideration that there is a significant non-uniform digital access to ICT between developed and developing countries (UN, 2007), and within nations, sustainability (i.e., access to ICT), reliability (such as, electricity, Internet), and equity of open education, and hence employment, remain problematic. For example, in countries where there is a low level of literacy, let alone digital literacy, access to open knowledge is restricted. Even when opportunity to use ICT is at hand, it requires initial investments such as hardware, software, expertise, time, and effort to create new knowledge, which typically are not recompensated immediately. The gap between generations may also increase, being that youths are often more daring and curious about trying new things, and are more motivated to use the new "canned" (i.e., the commercialized ready-to-consume software) and open technologies. Nyambe and Shipena (1998) talk about a North-South divide, where "the North is developed, industrialized, advanced, etc., while the South is the Third World, underdeveloped, less advanced, etc." (p. 2), which counteracts the idea of global community, rather meant to fuel an exploitative interdependence of nations in the global economy and to superficially reproduce the status quo. Another divide is between rural areas on one hand and urbanized, micropolitan, and metropolitan areas on the other hand, with the industrialized areas being more developed and valuing more education. This means that open education can further contribute to the deepening of the social divide in the globalized world. In this context, perhaps open education should be referred to as "quasi-open" education, opened for the higher classes and closed for the lower classes within nations, and opened for the developed countries and closed for the developing countries.

Nevertheless, the digital disconnect tends to fade, especially within Western countries, but also within and among the other nations. Thus the socio-economic gap between those with computer access is closing, in part because the older technologies become cheaper as newer technologies are developed, and new technologies develop faster and cheaper (Tomke, 2001) because free trade allows cheaper manufacturing of ICT devices, because many refurbished corporate ICT devices find uses in schools (e.g., Alexander, 2008), because more and more rural areas become urbanized due to industrialization (e.g., Kelly, 1998), and because the economic power is beginning to diffuse from the U.S. to Eastern Asia, Western Europe, Central Europe, and Russia (Bunke, 1990). This would mean that the worldwide connectivity will increase, facilitating the globalization of connectivity. By providing multiple perspectives, OP along with globalized trade, among other factors, should contribute to a decrease in ethno-centrism and nation-centrism, of localism and tradition-based identity, shaping the global citizenship identity and replacing it with a Westernized identity. In this context, we can speculate that OP contributes to the displacement of identity and secularization of nations, by invading and eventually changing the individual and national belief structures. Nevertheless, this technological inclusivity, leading eventually to an "Open Education for All' movement, must not be seen as inherently good or bad, but it is important to note how its use is negotiated on micro and global scales.

OPEN SOCIETY AND OPEN EDUCATION IN ROMANIA

Romania is situated in the South Eastern part of Europe, spanning a total surface of approximately 91,700 square miles, smaller then the state of Oregon (Internet World Stats, 2007). Historically, the Romanian people are the descendants of the native Dacians and the conquering Romans, explaining the name of the country and the Latin origin of the official language. Romanian is in fact the only Latin language in Eastern Europe. After becoming a unified country in 1918, Romania has known the following successive political regimes: monarchy until the 1930s, fascism until the 1940s, communism until 1989, and the recent transition to democracy. Romania joined NATO in 2004 and the EU in January 2007. Of the 22 million inhabitants of Romania, approximately 97% are literate (2005 Census). The percentage of Internet users in Romania has increased from 3.6 in 2000 to 22.1 in 2005, and to 32.4 in 2006 (World Development Indicators, 2007), mostly from the upper-middle income group, compared with 9.8% Internet users in Europe and in the Central Asia region. In 2006, there were seven secure Internet servers that connected 1 million Romanian users (World Bank, ICT, 2008).

Romania endured close to 50 years of communism and relative political isolation from democratic countries, when the cultural and educational exchanges were limited to then also communist countries or under some type of dictatorship, such as Russia, East Germany, Hungary, Poland, Bulgaria, China, North Korea, Libya, Iraq, or Vietnam. The Romanian society was under a general state of oppression imposed by the communist regime in Romania when the freedom of speech, democratic participation, and independent thinking were highly restricted. The sudden change of political regime that came with the People's Revolution of December 1989, lead the closed Romanian society to a type of freedom that the older generation forgot and the new generation never knew before. The Romanian people had to negotiate their own meaning of the democratic liberties within the specific Romanian context. Birzea (1996, p. 99) notes that in education, "after the first 'revolutionary' shock, there followed changing measures regarding curricula and textbooks, teaching methods and educational standards. Without affecting the structures and institutions, these reforms are the expression of a *catching-up policy*, of synchronisation with the West." In general, the educational and social policy became centred on the community, family, and child, rather than on the institution itself, as it had been before.

The collapse of the communist block in the 1990's has gotten the businessman and philanthropist George Soros interested in investing into the emerging open society in the South Eastern Europe (Open Society Institute, 2008). In Romania, among other things, the Soros Foundation collaborated with the Romanian Ministry of Education to contributing to endowing schools with computers and new technology and collaborating towards developing alternative textbooks (Soros Foundation Romania, 2007). Today, with the work of the Soros Foundation, Romania remains focused on education, civil society, communication, culture and health. Another foundation that encourages democratic and economic transition in Romania is the Fulbright Commission in Romania, established in 1993, by setting up scholarships for competitive and merituous students to study and experience the life on U.S. campuses (Fulbright Romania, 2007). The fact that Romania acceded to be a member of the European Union was a sign that the 17 years of democratic confusion and struggle were a good start for the building of a true democracy and towards becoming an open society. Romanians realized that advanced societies are open societies, and they are continuing to pursue the goal of freedom by being actively involved in the building of the new democratic society and contributing to the democratization of information in Romania.

Today, the open education is mainly framed through the four 'classic' international documents: Budapest Open Access Initiative (2001), Berlin Declaration on Open Access to Knowledge in the Sciences and Humanities (2003), Bethesda Statement on Open Access Publishing (2003), and Declaration of Salvador – Commitment to Equity (2005). The rise of Romanian open education initiatives for making available on the Internet of educational sources is timid because the websites are only partially corresponding to the conceptualization of open education. For example, *Didactic.ro* (2008) is a database of pedagogical materials, with partial reserved rights imposed; *Clopotel.ro* (2008) is a website exclusively with educational content games, contests, essays, Olympics questions and answers, etc.; *Bacalaureat2007.com* (2008) contains details, helpful materials, and a forum about the Baccalaureate exam, plus a page where the solutions to exams can be purchased; *Olimpiade.ro* (2008) contains a database of educational materials from the national Olympic examinations in various subjects, useful to both professors and students; and *Ecursuri.ro* (2008) promotes online classes on various topics, downloadable for free (Nae & Constantinescu, 2007). All these examples offer educational materials for downloading, but do not provide the possibility for modifying and uploading the files, however, feedback through forums and emails to website administrators is possible. The National Centre for Open Distance Education in Romania has branches in 8 main university centres and has the full support of 12 universities within the PHARE Programme for Multi-Country Cooperation for Distance Education.

Judging by Romania's experience of skill building in Cybernetics, by the fact that many software programmers and web designers are hired nowadays by top universities and corporations worldwide, and by the bad reputation that Romania has earned due to the high number of cyber crimes, it appears that Romania has the potential for developing constructive initiatives and human resource training related to open source and education. It was a Romanian, Stefan Odobleja, who first wrote about the principles of generalized cybernetics, being a forerunner of this field later established by the American Norbert Wiener (Biocrawler, 2005; Jurcau, 2008). Also, Odobleja (1938–1939, 1978) was the first scientist to introduce the 'law of reversibility', i.e. the principle of feedback, and discussed its importance in psycho-physiology, psycho-pathology, language, sociology, and aesthetics (Jurcau, 2008). Odobleja's work was forgotten until better use was made for Wiener's similar concepts and the field of cybernetics began to develop. Afterwards, the ex-Romanian dictator, Ceausescu, wanted to build a technologically modern Romania, so he encouraged software programming among other technical abilities (BBC News, 2003). These skills got Romanians noticed abroad, and because of the lack of reinforcement (small salary and narrow job spectrum) within their own country, many Romanians preferred to get jobs with various foreign software companies. Today it is unofficially said that Romanian is the second language spoken at the International Business Machines (IBM) Corporation because of the high number of Romanian skilled workers hired by this company (A World without Romania, 2008). The recent *2007 Internet Crime Report* places Romania fifth on the list of countries by the amount of perpetrators of online crime (Wikinews, 2008). Websites that reveal various mechanisms of cyber-crimes warn Internet users about Romanian fraudulent business schemes from eBay (e.g., Scams.Flipshark.Com, 2002). In December 2006, the leader of a Romanian hacker gang called the "WhiteHat Team" was charged with breaking into U.S. government computers belonging to the Navy, the Department of Energy, and NASA (e.g., Washkuch, 2006). Just recently, in April 2008, a well-known Romanian hacker was arrested in Bucharest for causing a damage of approximately $1 million to eBay clients (e.g., Goodin, 2008). The good news is that on one hand the Romanian police and secret service collaborate with foreign similar agencies to pin down these types of perpetrators, while on the other hand the Romanian government, universities, and private agencies strive to create a partnership in creating opportunities for open source. For example, the eLiberatica 2008 Conference has taken place at World Trade Center, Bucharest, Romania, bringing together all those interested in the "the benefits of Open and Free Technologies" (eLiberatica, 2008).

Despite the fact that in 2005, 57% of the Romanian schools were connected to the Internet (World Bank, ICT, 2008), like in other developing countries, most rural and even some urban schools in Romania lack the funding for acquiring ICT devices for students to use regularly. From previous experience, the internet connection is reserved for administrative staff to use because there are no filtering systems to simultaneously monitor the student's browsing history or block a student's attempt to access a non-educational site. The ICT training is therefore limited to certain strata of the population, contributing to the digital divide discussed in the previous section.

Most open source people are students, who feel under pressure to compete for jobs in a global world with students from advanced democratized countries, who have long had the access to open source education both in schools and at home. In addition to providing access to open education projects through providing infrastructure and safe guidelines to benefiting from the Internet resources, the educational system from Romania also needs to align to the challenge of demo-cratization of information, teaching students to learn independently (as opposed to only following the current standardized and rigid curricula) and take part of extracurricular activities (currently sporadically and scarcely organized in the Romanian schools), teaching students how to take the responsibility of acquiring new information, work in teams, and volunteer for their, virtual, or global community.

In the era of informationalism, the public Internet cafes from Bucharest and throughout the country are disappearing because they turned out not to be as profitable as the owners expected. In addition, currently there are no public places that offer wireless connection, leaving the people who want to access the Internet without any public facility to help them do so.

Besides lacking the infrastructure in terms of access to the open source, Romanian learners' full access to open education is also limited by the limited number of English speakers and/or proficient knowledge of the English language among the Romanians. English is spoken by approximately five million Romanians, many of whom are young (Wikipedia Romania, 2008).

THE PROMISE OF OPEN EDUCATION

Digital literacy is to become the literacy of the new millennium, as it becomes a necessity, not an option. Textbook-based literacy is shown insufficient to meet the realities and challenges of 21st century informational changes. Thus, informal education adds value to the traditional formal education for example by offering opportunities to start a business, launch a product, gain reputation, and add expertise. The development of open education depends therefore on the development of technology, which may take different forms. Technology will probably become more and more affordable for consumers and the development of a truly global human network will be easier to achieve in this way. As people become more transparent and open about their experiences, a trend already in progress, browsing the Internet will become an educational experience in itself. English will perhaps remain the lingua franca of the Internet, cementing the global network, but not necessarily the most used one, with languages spoken in large nations like Mandarin, Hindi, Spanish, Korean, and Russian gaining primacy (Anderson & Rainie, 2006). Given the prevalence of ICT, there will probably be more and more protests against the use of applied scientific knowledge and its influence on education and globalization. The danger of "ICT" dependency, technology isolation syndrome, or a type of autistic isolation from reality and the creation of a multimedia virtual reality is predicted to present a bigger threat in the future, resulting in less developed communication skills. With an innovational goal in mind, more money, time, and effort will probably be invested in technology and open education than ever before.

Education, in both the traditional view as school graduation and in the post-modernistic view of long life learning, has shifted its emphasis from social equality and mobility more towards social mobility and efficiency to fit the new global post-Keynesian economic integration and neo-liberal societies, "by producing efficient and effective workers to meet the requirements of the global economy" (Rizvi, Engel, Rutkowski, & Sparks, 2007, p. 7). Open education emphasizes so much more the production of efficient users, driven by the global market in a time dominated by rapid changes enabled by technology. The use of ICT, the dissemination of information in English as the primary language, the alteration of emphasis of education on efficiency, and the increased weight of international standardized testing (such as PISA, 2005 and TIMMS, 2008) suggests a move towards a possible global standards within the education curriculum.

Because ICT mediates our existence and permeates especially informal education, where the flood of information is one click away, we need to develop methods of teaching about the possible misuses of information, to teach learners how to develop internal restraints from using information in certain circumstances (e.g., how to use weapons, how to hack into a website), and to emphasize teaching social skills to minimize or compensate for the negative effects of the overuse of technology. These ought to be valid statements for all societies, especially for young democracies like Romania, where democracy is partially misunderstood and still loosely regulated in legal terms.

We saw that Romania can offer a human resources pool to the advancement of the open source market, but what is the future of open source in Romania? Romania, society in general, and the governmental institutions, would benefit greatly from open source because the financial means to acquire software licenses is limited, therefore, selling services would be a good start for the Romanian companies. Open source will provide Romanians with a new heuristic paradigm of thinking, where there is no one solution but multiple or no solution at all. Open source would also contribute to the changing of the teaching and learning styles in

Romanian schools as discussed earlier, especially considering experiencing peer to peer collaboration (peer training and peer modelling) as a vital mechanism to advancing the democratization process within the Romanian society.

Time is an important dimension to how OP will develop in the future because changes in important elements of OP such as demographic structure of learners, learners' belief systems, and global and local development of all kinds can be highly influenced by even a short period of time. In time, OP can represent an alternative to the globalization movement through all its benefits discussed throughout this chapter, including creation and distribution of information in more rapid and wider fashion; bridging the educational achievement gap between North and South, developed and developing, high and low class, urban and rural areas, etc.; decentralizing and democratizing information, thus reducing commercial monopolies; and create versatile human capital to compete in the global knowledge economy.

The promise of open education rests with its benefits and with its rapid and increasingly spread among the ICT users. This is how globalization gained dominance over the world's mechanisms, also. It is possible for the open source to become a "disruptive innovation" (Bower & Christensen, 1995) or rather, a 'disruptive education', that is, a type of education that does not remain necessarily revolutionary, but can overturn the dominant existing type of education by successively moving up in the market through performance improvements until finally displaces the current formal education. Is it possible for open education to take over traditional education by the end of the 21st century? I believe it is very unlikely, but if new ways of profit and productivity will be embedded within it or linked to it, other than charging for the educational services, then in the next centuries it is possible that only knowledge itself and its functionality will be appreciated globally, with no need to produce proof of attendance of any traditional type of school (not even of the compulsory school years). For example, Saedi (2003) describes the Internet and Computing Core Certification (IC³) as "the first global Internet and computing literacy measurement standard", which was launched on February 2002, and is now used in over 60 countries. "IC³ provides a common entry-level qualification that individuals around the world can aspire to possess, in a step to foster true equal opportunities for those cultures and economies eager to be part of the information revolution."

We can speculate that there is the possibility for international standardized entrance-job tests to be commercially developed and globally used by transnational, international, and global corporations in the next decades. These tests can give the employer an idea about the abilities of a potential employee who may reside on the other side of the globe or who was trained in another country. The employee may pay a modest fee for the "processing" of such a test, and open education will have a legitimate play in the globalization process, contributing to the perpetuation of the hegemonic few. However, I believe that in education there will always be a need for redundancy, similar to the industrial redundancy where "back-up" pieces are built in the system that would automatically pick up the work of the ones that fail. Learners would benefit more of a comprehensive type of education, where human input is possible and needed. And then again, it is possible that some other form of education, probably also technologically-based, will develop in the next centuries and there will be a need for re-negotiating towards a new and more fluid type of education.

REFERENCES

A World without Romania. (2008). *YouTube: A world without Romania Hi-res*. Retrieved May 3, 2008, from http://www.youtube.com/watch?v=oEH2gh-zsxM

Alexander, S. (2008). *A Bayport nonprofit gets refurbished corporate computers into schools*. Retrieved May 1, 2008, from http://www.startribune.com/business/13852426.html

Anderson, J. Q., & Rainie, L. (2006). *The future of the internet II: PEW project & American life project*. Retrieved April 25, 2008, from http://www.pewInternet.org/pdfs/PIP_Future_of_Internet_2006.pdf

Appadurai, A. (2007). Disjuncture and difference in the global cultural economy. In J. X. Inda & R. Rosaldo (Eds.), *The antropology of globalization: A reader* (pp. 27–47). Oxford; Malden, MA: Blackwell Publishing.

Bacalaureat2007.com. (2008). *Bacalaureat: Bac pe paine [Baccalaureate on bread]*. Retrieved April 30, 2008, from http://www.bacalaureat2007.com/

Barab, S. (2001). *Ecological paradigm: Seeing a new model of learning*. Retrieved March 20, 2008, from http://inkido.indiana.edu/research/theory.html

BBC News. (2003). *Romania tackles rise in cyber-crime*. Retrieved May 2, 2008, from http://news.bbc.co.uk/2/hi/technology/3344721.stm

Beckett, D., & Hager, P. J. (2002). *Life, work and learning: Practice and postmodernity*. Independence, KY: Routledge.

Benkler, Y. (2003). The political economy of commons. *The European Journal for the Informatics Professional, IV*(3), 6–9.

Berlin Declaration. (2003). *Berlin declaration on open access to knowledge in the sciences and humanities*. Retrieved April 30, 2008, from http://oa.mpg.de/openaccess-berlin/berlindeclaration.html

Bethesda Statement. (2003). *Bethesda statement on open access publishing*. Retrieved April 30, 2008, from http://www.earlham.edu/%7Epeters/fos/bethesda.htm

Biocrawler. (2005). *Biocrawler.com: Stefan Odobleja*. Retrieved May 3, 2008, from http://www.biocrawler.com/w/index.php?title=Stefan_Odobleja&redirect=no

Bower, J. L., & Christensen, C. M. (1995). Disruptive technologies: Catching the wave. *Harvard Business Review, 73*, 43–53.

Birzea, C. (1996). Educational reform and power struggles in Romania. *European Journal of Education, 31*, 97–107.

Budapest Open Access Initiative. (2001). *Budapest open access initiative: Home*. Retrieved April 30, 2008, from http://www.soros.org/openaccess/index.shtml

Bunke, H. C. (1990). Pax Americana – Forecast for U.S. economic power. *Business Horizons*. Retrieved May 1, 2008, from http://findarticles.com/p/articles/mi_m1038/is_n1_v33/ai_8880687

Cape Town Open Education Declaration. (2007). *Cape Town open education declaration: Unlocking the promise of open educational resources*. Retrieved March 19, 2008, from http://www.capetowndeclaration.org/read-the-declaration

CISCO. (2008). *Corporate overview: Research and development*. Retrieved March 19, 2008, from http://newsroom.cisco.com/dlls/corpinfo/corporate_overview.html

CISCO IBSG. (2007). *21st century trends for higher education*. CISCO: Wilen-Daugenti, T. Retrieved March 19, 2008, from http://www.hedtrends.com/hed/papers/Top%20trends%20in%20Education%20White%20Paper.pdf

CISCO Systems Inc. (2007). *Welcome to the human network at work: CISCO Systems Inc., 2007 annual report*. Retrieved March 19, 2008, from http://www.cisco.com/web/about/ac49/ac20/downloads/annualreport/ar2007/pdf/cisco_ar2007_complete.pdf

CISCO. (2008, January). *Equipping every leaner for the 21st century: CISCO whitepaper.* Paper presented at the World Economic Forum, Switzerland, Davos.

Clopotel.ro. (2008). *Clopoţel.ro [Bell.ro].* Retrieved April 30, 2008, from http://www.clopotel.ro/

Declaration of Salvador. (2005). *Declaration of Salvador - Commitment to equity.* Retrieved March 19, 2008, from http://www.icml9.org/channel.php?lang=en&channel=91&content=438

Didactic.ro. (2008). *Didactic.ro: Cancelaria Natională [National Teacher's Room].* Retrieved April 30, 2008, from http://www.didactic.ro/

Dholakia, U. M., King, W. J., & Baraniuk, R. (2006). *What makes an open education program sustainable? The case of connections.* Retrieved March 20, 2008, from http://www.oecd.org/dataoecd/3/6/36781781.pdf

Ecursuri.ro. (2008). *Cursuri, referate, teste şi jocuri gratuite [Free courses, essays, tests, and games].* Retrieved May 4, 2008, from http://ecursuri.ro/

eLiberatica. (2008). *eLiberatica 2008 – The benefits of open and free technologies.* Retrieved May 4, 2008, from http://eliberatica.ro/2008/index

Everett, D. R. (2002). Technology and effective communication. *National Business Education Yearbook, 40,* 227–244.

Fryer, W. A. (2004). Digital literacy NOW! *Teach Learning.* Retrieved April 24, 2008, from http://www.techlearning.com/showArticle.php?articleID=18902855

Fulbright Romania. (2007). *Fulbright Romania.* Retrieved May 4, 2008, from http://www.fulbright.ro/

Goodin, D. (2008). Notorious eBay hacker arrested in Romania: Vladuz impaled. *The Register.* Retrieved May 3, 2008, from http://www.theregister.co.uk/2008/04/18/vladuz_arrested/

Hafner, K., & Lyon, M. (1996). *Where wizards stay up late: The origins of the internet.* New York: Simon & Schuster.

Heylighen, F. (2007). Why is open access development so successful? Stigmergic organization and the economics of information. In B. Lutterbeck, M. Barwolff, & R. A. Gehring (Eds.), *Open source* (pp. 1–12). Jahrbuch: Lehmanns Media. Retrieved March 20, 2008, from http://learn.ed.uiuc.edu/mod/resource/view.php?inpopup=true&id=14924

Information for Development Program. (2005, March). *Knowledge maps: ICTs in education.* Washington, DC: Trucano, M. Retrieved March 20, 2008, from http://www.ictliteracy.info/rf.pdf/KnowledgeMaps_ICTs_and_the_Education_MDGs.pdf

Internet World Stats. (2007). *European Union.* Retrieved December 7, 2007, from http://www.internetworldstats.com/europa.htm#ro

Isaacson, D. (2002). Instant information gratification. *American Libraries, 33*(2), 39.

Jurcau, N. (2008). Two specialists in cybernetics: Stefan Odobleja and Norbert Weiner. Common and different features. *Paidea – Comparative Philosophy.* Retrieved May 3, 2008, from http://www.bu.edu/wcp/Papers/Comp/CompJurc.htm

Kelly, P. F. (1998). The politics of urban-rural relations: Land use conversion in the Philippines. *Environment and Urbanization, 10,* 35–54. Retrieved April 30, 2008, from http://eau.sagepub.com/cgi/reprint/10/1/35.pdf

Legrain, P. (2003, May 9). Cultural globalization is not Americanization. *The Chronicle of Higher Education - The Chronicle Review, 49*(35), B7.

Marchand, D., & Horton, F. (1986). *Infotrend: Profiting from your information sources.* New York: Wiley.

Nae, R., & Constantinescu, N. (2007). *Drumul către Cape Town – Educaţie Deschisă [The pathway towards Cape Town – Open education].* Retrieved March 21, April 30, 2008, from http://www.olimpiade.ro/data/drumulcatrecapetown.pdf

Naughton, J. (2000). *A brief history of the future.* Woodstock; New York: The Overlook Press.

Nyambe, J., & Shipena, I. (1998). Global education on the threshold of a new millennium. *Reform Forum: Journal for Educational Reform in Namibia, 7,* 1–6.

Odobleja, S. (1938–1939). *Psychologie consonantiste [Consonantist psychology].* Paris: Librairie Maloine.

GABRIELA WALKER

Odobleja, S. (1978). *Psihologia consonantistă şi cibernetica [Consonantist psychology and cybernetics]*. Craiova: Editura Scrisul Românesc.

Olimpiade.ro. (2008). *Olimpiade.ro [Olympiads]*. Retrieved April 30, 2008, from http://www.olimpiade.ro/

Open Society Institute. (2008). *Open society institute & Soros foundation network: Building a global alliance for open society – Overview.* Retrieved May 4, 2008, from http://www.soros.org/about/overview

Petraglia, L. (1998). *Reality by design: The rhetoric and technology of authenticity in education.* Mahwah, NJ: Lawrence Erlbaum Associates.

Pisha, B., & Coyne, P. (2001). Smart from the start: The promise of universal design for learning. *Remedial and Special Education, 22*(4), 197–203.

Peters, M. A. (2007). The political economy of informational democracy. *Global Knowledge Cultures,* 209–221.

PISA. (2005). *Programme for international student assessment.* Retrieved March 21, 2008, from http://www.pisa.oecd.org/dataoecd/15/13/39725224.pdf

Pisha, B., & Coyne, P. (2001). Smart from the start: The promise of universal design for learning. *Remedial and Special Education, 22*(4), 197–203.

Rizvi, F., Engel, L., Rutkowski, D., & Sparks, J. (2007). Equality and the politics of globalization in education. In G. K. Verma, C. R. Bagley, & M. M. Jha (Eds.), *International perspectives on educational diversity and inclusion: Studies from America, Europe, and India* (pp. 3–20). New York: Routledge.

Saedi, D. (2003). Digital global literacy white paper/Bylined article. *Global Digital Literacy Council.* Retrieved May 4, 2008, from http://www.gdlcouncil.org/gdlc_byline.html

Scams.Flipshark.Com. (2002). *The Romanian laptop scam.* Retrieved May 3, 2008, from http://scams.flipshark.com/rcscam.html

Steger, M. B. (2003). *Globalization: A very short introduction.* Oxford: University Press.

Sleeman, P., & Rockwell, D. (Eds.). (1981). *Designing learning environments.* New York: Longman.

Soros Foundation Romania. (2007). *Soros foundation Romania: Home.* Retrieved May 4, 2008, from http://www.osf.ro/en/index.php

TIMMS. (2008). *Trends in International Mathematics and Science Study.* Retrieved March 21, 2008, from http://nces.ed.gov/timss/

Tomke, S. (2001). Enlightened experimentation: The new imperative for innovation. *Harvard Business Review, 79*(2), 67–75.

UN. (2007). *Millennium development goals indicators: The official United Nations site for the MDG indicators.* Retrieved March 21, 2008, from http://mdgs.un.org/unsd/mdg/default.aspx

UNESCO. (2007). Open educational resources: The way forward. In S. D'Antoni (Ed.), *UNESCO, International Institute for Educational Planning.* Retrieved March 20, 2008, from http://oerwiki.iiep-unesco.org/images/4/46/OER_Way_Forward.pdf

Washkuch, F. Jr. (2006). Feds charge Romanian hacker for cracking NASA, Navy networks. *SC Magazine.* Retrieved May 3, 2008, from http://www.scmagazineus.com/Feds-charge-Romanian-hacker-for-cracking-NASA-Navy-networks/article/34191/

Webopedia. (2006). *The birth of the internet.* Retrieved October 15, 2006, from http://www.webopedia.com/DidYouKnow/Internet/2002/BirthoftheInternet.asp

Wikinews. (2008). *UK nears US in cyber-crime, ahead of Nigeria, Romania.* Retrieved May 3, 2008, from http://en.wikinews.org/wiki/UK_nears_US_in_cyber-crime,_ahead_of_Nigeria,_Romania

Wikipedia Romania. (2008). *Romania.* Retrieved March 20, 2008, from http://en.wikipedia.org/wiki/Romania

World Bank, ICT. (2008). *World Bank, Romania: ICT at a glance.* Retrieved April 30, 2008, from http://devdata.worldbank.org/ict/rom_ict.pdf

World Development Indicators. (2007). *Romania data profile: World development indicators database.* Retrieved April 30, 2008, from http://devdata.worldbank.org/external/CPProfile.asp?PTYPE= CP&CCODE=ROM

Gabriela Walker, Ed. S.
Global Studies in Education,
University of Illinois at Urbana-Champaign

LUCINDA MORGAN

8. SPREADING THE FLAME BEFORE THE BLAZE CAN BE EXTINGUISHED

Open Source, Open Access, and Online Education in the People's Republic of China

INTRODUCTION

Tiananmen. Taiwan. Tibet. Most "foreigners"[1] who have visited the Peoples Republic of China are cautioned to avoid bringing up these topics with Chinese they encounter in the Mainland. Foreign students who study Chinese culture are mystified as to why these three "T's" are so taboo, as are non-Chinese citizens who work in China, as a common appendix to their employment contracts includes clauses instructing them to never initiate discussions about these matters with their local co-workers. Another "forbidden" topic, though not often mentioned in international media, is Xinjiang, the most western province of China, which borders Pakistan, Afghanistan, and Kazakstan, and has a predominately Muslim native population. The most recent of this divisive, prohibited list is an event that is traditionally considered to be a jubilant occasion for the world to unite together and display its ultimate athletic abilities: the 2008 summer Olympics, which will be hosted by Beijing. At different points in history, the Olympics have been used as a forum for certain groups and causes to exhibit their displeasure regarding political or social movements[2]. The recent protests involving China's hosting of the Olympics are usually in regards to accusations of human rights violations, notably in Tibet against Buddhist monks, but also for a varied list of other reasons. Forms of protest have included attempts to disrupt the global voyage of the Olympic torch and demonstrations, both within China and internationally. It is reasonable to assume that given the amount of time, energy, and money China's government has invested in the upcoming Olympics, along with the great sense of pride they have with their world gazing upon their country's greatness, the government is not pleased with the negative publicity that has been generated.

One of the consequences of this worldwide attention is that the Chinese government has been more active in blocking, or censoring, of information available to the general, domestic population. The internet, through the World Wide Web, is a major source of information gathering and knowledge exchange that is accessible throughout the world, given that one has a computer with functioning connection capabilities. With the vast amount of information available at one's fingertips, it is inevitable that while much of what is available is informative, some will be of a negative persuasion, depending on one's perspective

M.A. Peters and R.G. Britez (eds.), Open Education and Education for Openness, 95–104.
© *2008 Sense Publishers. All rights reserved.*

or vantage point. Governing a population in excess of a billion people is no easy task, and the Chinese government typically goes about it by promoting a strong sense of nationalism among its constituents. As such, this nationalism often is extended to a point that certain "forbidden" areas are not to be known about, much less discussed as conversation or debate topics within China, for the risk that they shine a harmful light upon the government. The internet contains information, pictures, and videos outlining these taboo areas, but these topics, including entire websites, are generally blocked in China when one tries to access the information via search engines or other methods. Hindering access to internet websites is not a new practice in China. On his Open Access News website, Peter Suber notes on September 3, 2002, China blocked access to Google because it "brings up too many links to censored sites" (Suber 2002). Other sites that have been blocked sporadically within China include Wikipedia, Yahoo, and MSN. While China has been preoccupied in its Olympic preparations in recent years, many worldwide developments involving the internet have also been progressing. Movements towards collaborations on software development, combining information resources via online publishing, and making online educational experiences more accessible are areas in which the internet is vital. China, though not the world leader in these areas, has been apt to associate itself with these developments, quite often through the encouragement and funding by the government. It is commendable that the government has dedicated resources towards these projects, and advances have occurred as a result. This paper outlines the history, current situation, and projected challenges concerning open source, open access, and online education in China. It also details areas in which the Chinese government is involved in such endeavors, and inquires as to how a government can attempt to be progressive in technological movements that involve access to information by way of the internet, while at the same time limiting and blocking knowledge sources to its own population that the rest of the world can see.

OPEN SOURCE

Red Flag Linux[3] is given credit for being the first successful open source software in China. Established in 1999, it is a *Linux* operating system that is designed and distributed as a government initiative by the Software Research Institute of the Chinese Academy of Sciences[4]. The Software Research Institute is a government institution in which nearly all the members are from the same institutions and are usually even physically grouped together. Though Guohan Pan and Curtis Bonk (2007) report in their research that there is not any public information about the group, they suspect the development team is set-up in a hierarchical manner, due to the members already belonging to established structures. They go on to ration that this system leads to a higher level of efficiency, as well as more highly effective than a non-institutional, open source movement that is not as well-organized (p. 3). China's first open source software organization, the Software Promotion Alliance, was founded in 2004, with the purpose of collaborating efforts in *Linux* development, encouraging open source development and usage in China, and leading exchanges and support systems for open source communities in northeast Asia. The Chinese software companies involved with this project included *Red Flag Software, Beijing Co-Create open-source, Zhongbiao Software, Wuxi Evermore Software, Kingsoft, Beijing Redflag Chinese 2000*, as well as the international partners of *IBM, Hewlett-Packard, Intel*, and *Novell* (p. 2).

Reasons for the Chinese Government's support for open source software includes the lower cost involved, the benefits to local industries, and as Marson suggests in the article "China: Local Software for Local People", possible "distrust of American imperialism" (Pan & Bonk, 2007, p. 4). Despite the widespread availability of *Microsoft Windows*, currently in China, roughly 30 percent of desktops computers use *Linux* ("Desktop battle", qtd. in Pan & Bonk, 2007, p. 3). Some members of the Chinese Government believe in a conspiracy theory of sorts that the United States Government has implanted codes in *Microsoft* software, which they could direct and control China's computing infrastructure. Governments at all levels in China utilize *Red Flag Linux*, ranging from such divisions as China Post, China Tobacco, the Public Security and China Banking Regulatory Commission, and the Custom General Office. With this wide range of government services using *Red Flag Linux*, its evident to see how integrated it is and one can speculate how much of an influence the state has in its future development, and as Pan admits in his article "The Emergence of Open-Source Software in China," "the future for *Red Flag Linux* looks very bright in China" (p. 3).

According to an article written by Bob Liu in 2002, China is emerging as "one of the world's strongholds for the *Linux* operating system. He went on to report that the results from a study by Evans Data showed that two-thirds of computer programmers within China would work using *Linux* in the upcoming year. The same study also predicted that the use of *Linux* as the primary host operating system was expected to jump by 175 percent by 2003. Esther Schindler, an analyst for Evans Data, pointed out that their research indicated a large shift in operating system preferences in China, which she felt was a response to the government's promotional efforts to adopt *Linux* (Liu, 2002).

Showing evidence of China's enthusiasm for open source, the 2007 China Open Source Software Summit was held in Beijing in March (2007)[5]. In its initial phases prior to the conference, organizations hoped that the conference would be an opportunity to publicly promote the concept of open source, so they set up nine districts throughout the country, and included governments, companies, and academies. Examples of their outreach efforts included speaking at schools to attract students and teachers to learn more about the open source industry, and setting up panels in cities with substantial I.T. industries to discuss such topics as licenses, tools, and other open source issues (Yang, 2007).

At the conference, which China's Co-Create Software League (Cosoft)[6] software sponsored, twenty-five winners out of fifty-three applications were awarded prizes in the contest. Winners included Sun Changzheng, for his Shuangjie Chinese Input Platform[7]. Not all participants at the conference agreed with Cosoft and government officials who praised the contest as successful. A Chinese open source supporter disagreed with the praises, though he realized it was good advertisement for the movement, because he felt strongly that the contest was sponsored by "organizers who violate the principles of open source" (Yang, 2007). The individual, who asked to remain anonymous, criticized their lack of knowledge of open source software, because "unlike the government projects they're used to, open source software comes from community efforts. We keep improving it by feedback from other programmers and users. But the [contest] organizer seemed to ask for only 'finished' software" (Yang, 2007).

John Howkins, a leading British expert in the creative industries, would agree with this, as he is happy with the progress China has made in recent years, though he considers the future should strive for a better balance with public ownership. He also recommends that China better manage copyright laws, as it is a major importer of creative projects. In an interview with China Business Weekly, Howkins advised, "you won't import creative goods until you have a law...China must have a strict law, especially the enforcement of the law at local levels," which would require involvement from the government. To this regard, also warns that China should not prevent public access in the process of protecting creative industries, but should rather develop education programs that would teach people about copyrights and sharing information, as he predicts that "the future of China lies in the brain...(so) intellectual freedom is a necessity" ("What should").

The open source movement has also fostered a drive towards additional nationalism in China, as *Microsoft* is viewed as a monopolistic Western system, whereas *Red Flag Linux* (and other domestic software products) use "millions of talented, university-educated individuals in its quest to develop its own brand of copyrighted software" (Pan & Bonk, 2007, p. 4). The sheer number of university students and graduates who are able to combine their efforts through open source and collaborate on their programming enables China to maximize its expenses, and perpetuate its technology at a rate which could soon outpace that of countries that are currently more advanced in their projects. A related topic to nationalism in relation to China and open source applications is that of *localization*. Pan labels *localization* as a term that is "used by Chinese to mean the customization of software into Chinese" (5). As China strives to be a leader in open source, the progression of the concept of localization will be interesting to monitor, as programs are consumed from other sources and redesigned using Chinese as the language medium, thus reflecting the government's desire to maintain a strong sense of nationalism. This hidden undertone of nationalism combined with software development, while beneficial to China as a nation, can be contentious, as some will argue it goes against the global efforts to share universally. In addition, it reasserts the government's dominance concerning what is accessible to the common population, which is the root of the conflicts regarding Beijing's hosting of the summer Olympics.

Other areas in which China has become involved with the open source movement include the OpenCourseWare Consortium[8], which includes members from over sixteen countries, plus an additional fourteen affiliate organizations. Under the non-profit organization group CORE, China is the largest participant in the OpenCourseWare Consortium, with over thirty colleges involved in 2007

("How the open"). CORE's three main purposes include "introducing and promoting the use of MIT OCW universities across China, translating OCW, and launching CORE's website,"[9] whose mission "is to promote closer interaction and open sharing of educational resources between Chinese and international universities such as the OCW network" ("Open Education").

Some of the challenges facing the open source movement in China include the limited availability of domestically produced open source software; very little research concerning any established, domestic, open source communities; the viewpoint that many Chinese educational institutions share that open source software is just a substitute to expensive proprietary software; and language issues.

The language issues[10] involved include, but are not limited to, condensing the thousands of Chinese characters to a more manageable system, the absence of a standard alphabetic system, and the imperfections of instant translating engines (Yeates, 2005). Consequently, the open source development has also allowed for an answer to some of China's other pressing difficulties, as it is effective at addressing the issues of piracy, security, and high cost. And the more promising feature of open source is that has provided a means for more accessibility of knowledge and information resources for the general public, notably higher education, with an emphasis on programs for online distance learning (Pan & Bonk, 2007, p. 4). In actual numbers, there are more universities involved with open source in China than all of North America combined, and most would agree that China's current situation is lagging behind about five to seven years to that of North America (p. 9).

OPEN ACCESS

Open access is in its beginning stages in China, as Conghui Fang and Xiaochun Zhu's article notes that their paper is most likely the first research paper which outlines the status of open access in China. The term itself, open access, is new to the Chinese vocabulary, as the "International Conference on Strategies and Policies on Open Access to Scientific Information," held in Beijing in 2005, and is regarded as the birth of the movement in China. Fang and Zhu's research found that overall, most Chinese scholars support open access "principle that the published output of scientific research should be available without charge to everyone, and both author-pays publishing models and those which are self-archived are supported (p. 186). At current, there are only a few open access websites in China, and can be divided into two categories: original and transferred.

According to Fang and Zhu (2006), original websites "provide a network interface which allows writers to publish freely and readers to download freely," which allows for both quality and lesser quality papers to appear due to a lack of quality control, such as a peer-review system; consequently, these open access websites are not always an accurate source for information (p. 187). Chinese open access websites that use the original method include Qiji.cn, the Chinese Preprint Service System, and Sciencepaper Online[11]. With transferred works, the quality is considered higher based on the reputation and authority of the journal in which it is published and because of the established peer-review process which takes place prior to publishing. Examples include the alliance of Open Access Journals (OAJs)[12], whose goals are to "increase academic communication, increase transactions (especially among universities), (and) influence and promote open access," as well as individual open access journals through the Directory of Open Access Journals (DOAJ) [4] (p. 187). Another example, in the science field of Chinese information available via open access, is the China Gateway for the BioMed Central Open Access Publisher. The website contains articles written and co-written by researchers from China, Taiwan, Hong Kong, Macau that are published in the more than 160 open access journals available through the BioMed Central. Downloadable versions are available in both Mandarin and English, as well as promotional materials that explain the benefits for sharing materials using BioMed Central ("China Gateway").

As with any development, unforeseeable complications arise and future difficulties can be predicted. Fang and Zhu (2006) outline three hurdles they foresee in the future of China's open access movement: quality, outlay, and copyright. As with any open access system, quality is a key issue, as the quick, free features of it can quickly release information, both accurate and misleading. This is not an ideal solution to this problem, even though the traditional method of peer-review can help alleviate some of these faults, because traditional publishers are not always willing to commit to these conditions. With outlay, China currently does not have adequate funds for research, so it relies heavily upon funds from the government to obtain finances for building and maintaining the website infrastructure, as well as publication fees (p. 188).

Copyright is a concern in China in many spheres, and the open access movement must stress the importance of respect to intellectual property rights that are even more essential in this age of globalization. While the concept of copyright might seem to be acquired more quickly by Western countries, China has no history of it within its traditional culture. Confucius described the role of the writer a messenger rather than a creator, and that the writer should have benevolence for those writers before him. This notion of repeating the ancients has been instilled throughout the culture, and it will take a lot of effort and education in order to ensure that research being published by Chinese scholars is original, or at the very least, properly cited (Fang & zhu, 2006, p. 188).

ONLINE EDUCATION

China's Ministry of Education prefers to use the term "modern distance education"[13] rather than online education, as it highlights "the technological element employed by this mode of education" (Wang, 2006). China's first distance education program began in 1996, with four universities participating: Peking University, Qinghua University, Beijing Telecommunication University, and Hunan University[14]. China's first online educational standards for trial use were issued in 2000. Under the Ministry of Education's guidance, the Modern Distance Education Standardization Committee was responsible for creating guidelines that were applied to the 38 colleges and universities that were approved by 2000, which included approximately 160,000 students. At that time, the goal of having all primary and middle schools connected within five to ten years was also announced ("China issues"). Financial investments for online education in China have become a popular trend for investors, as the field of online education spreads across the country.

> *Education, throughout most of China's history, has been held with very high regard. Due to its geographical vastness, online education presented a miraculous opportunity for many in isolated and remote areas, though the reality was that in its infant stages, those areas were not wired and ready for the connections that were necessary to connect online educational opportunities. Despite this, the demand for online education in China has encountered different phases, while still expanding at an enormous rate. Not able to deal with all the technological demands and lack of initial regulations itself, beginning in 2003, the Ministry of Education began allowing separate organizations to handle procedures relating to their specific organizations (Wang & Crook, 2006).*

Students in rural areas are more likely to take advantage of online opportunities, as well as those who have did not pass the university entrance examinations, which one could assume indicates the caliber of the average online student is below that of those who were admitted to university under the traditional system. Another group of students who have taken advantage of online educational opportunities include those currently working who are looking to acquire new knowledge and skills, thus contributing to their lifelong education and training. As of 2006, though China is still in beginning trial stages of modern distance education, the Ministry of Education has given permission to sixty-eight schools of higher learning and the Central Radio and TV University. With nearly one and a half million students involved, there were over two thousand off-campus learning centers throughout the country offering forty majors for study ("Online").

As with other countries, one of the major factors contributing to the spread of distance education in China is the increasing availability of broadband technology. The CERNET (China Education and Research Network, which began in 1994, is currently the second largest Internet network in China; with over twenty-eight international and regional channels and reaching all the major cities, it is a high-speed transmission network of over twenty thousand kilometers. According to Wang and Crook's article, China has in place the infrastructure for modern distance education. The China Education and Research Network (CERNET) was established in 1994, and has expanded into an operative education network with three levels, which include the national level backbone network, local area networks (LANs), and campus intranets. In March 2004, the trial of the CERNET 2 project was performed, which connected dozens of universities across China. The difference between CERNET 1 and 2 is the use of IPv6 protocol, thus CERNET 2 offers transmissions speeds that are a thousand time faster than its predecessor. Other advantages include additional storage space, higher levels of security, better quality for synchronous communication, and a more convenient systems for end users The implementation of this technology has greatly aided the further development of modern distance education in China (Wang & Crook, 2006). In 2000, with the establishment of China Education Broadband Satellite Net, a "space to earth" transmission platform for modern distance education was launched, which allowed for a complete network support environment for distance education ("Online").

The financial benefits for a university to offer online educational opportunities are quite attractive, as China allows universities to seek external funding for their programs. Foreign and domestic investors are permitted to form partnerships with the approved universities and establish online institutes within the universities. As of August 2004, nearly two billion RMB had been invested in online education and over twelve billion RMB had been generated in revenue, thus making online education a very profitable venture for investors and the institutions. The online programs at the universities were funded either by joint funding with domestic technological companies or through sole funding (Wang & Crook, 2006).

One of the major challenges to online education in China was that there was not a coordinated national approach; rather there were as many versions of learning systems in place as there were schools involved (sixty-eight). Frustrated by the lack of consistency and organization, eight online institutions formed a consortium and signed the Taihu Declaration in August 2004. Because of this association, it was a precedent for future institutions to combine efforts and increase sharing amongst each other. Another major battle that has plagued online education is that of certification, both in regards to quality and the nature of the certification, and by both the general population and potential employers. Though, like in many other countries, there are three levels of higher education degrees[15] available through online coursework, the distrust was due to the varying standards of what each meant—there was not one set, regulated standard (Wang & Crook, 2006).

CONCLUSION

The developments of open source, open access, and online education do indeed have promising futures in China. It is also foreseeable that China will play a larger role in the future in these areas, as more developers and programmers get involved, and as the internet becomes more accessible in more remote areas in the country. This is an optimistic prospect, but one that could be hindered by should the government become too controlling in its interactions, just as many around the world would agree is happening with the current situation involving the Olympics. In order to participate and compete in the worldwide movement of technological advances, people must have access to information; that which is positive, and also the negative. Within China, the censorship of internet sites limits access—being denied the opportunity to view news on yahoo.com and contribute to Wikipedia, Chinese are flocking to sites that only provoke a façade of nationalism—one that that they are not able to critically examine because they have nothing to compare it to. By giving the public the availability to seek and search, the government is providing the tools for independent thought and creation, both of which are crucial in China's future developments of open source, open access, and online education. The motto of the Beijing Olympics is truly "one world, one dream"; it is time for the Chinese population to be exposed to all that there is to know in our shared world—so that they may have more have more of an opportunity to understand what it is that the rest of the world has been dreaming, and that they may have avenues by which they can build upon what is established and contribute to it as well.

NOTES

[1] "Foreigners" is the term used in Chinese Mandarin, 老外 or 外国人 (pronounced using pinyin as *laowai* or *waiguoren*) to indicate that a person is not native to China, usually based on their physical appearance (i.e. skin color). Within China, "foreigners" are usually tourists, exchange students, language teachers, or expatriates employed by international companies.

[2] The article "Long History of Olympic Protests," available on the BBC website (<http://news.bbc.co.uk/2/hi/europe/7334362.stm>, provides a detailed account of the protests and boycotts in recent history.

[3] The Chinese (pinyin) name for *Red Flag Linux* is 'Zhong Ke Hong Qi'. For more information, please consult <http://www.redflag-linux.com/eindex.html>.

[4] More detailed information regarding China's relation to *Linux* can be found at the China OSS Promotion Union's website: <http://www.oss.org.cn/en/index.php?option=com_frontpage& Itemid=1>.

[5] The first China Open Source Software Contest was held in 2004.

[6] Cosoft is associated with the semi-official Chinese Software Industry Association (CSIA). In a joint regulation with Double Software Certification (DSC), it is stated that if software is not improved by DSC for the CSIA, it cannot be sold in China. This policy is criticized by many Chinese individuals who support open source, as they view it as a huge obstacle that goes against basic principles of development.

[7] Programs for more effectively and efficiently imputing Chinese characters are crucial to the open source movement, as is discussed in a later paragraph.

[8] A by-product of MIT's OER initiative, the OpenCourseWare Consortium's growth rate indicates its clear success in the educational field.

[9] CORE's website can be accessed at this link: < http://www.core.org.cn/en/about_core/core_zl.html>.

[10] This issues pertaining to language and software production is not limited to China, but also plagues Korea and Japan, as they also use character-based writing systems.

[11] The websites for these are www.qiji.cn/; http://prep.istic.ac.cn; and www.paper.edu.cn.

[12] The website for Open Access Journals is www.oajs.org.

[13] In Mandarin Chinese (pinyin), it is pronounced as "xian dai yuan cheng jiao yu."

[14] The first three (Peking, Qinghua, and Beijing Telecommunications) universities are located in Beijing, while Hunan University is located in Hunan Province.

[15] The three levels being the diploma, graduate, and post-graduate levels. In addition, a certificate or degree can be given with successful completion of any of the programs.

BIBLIOGRAPHY

BioMed Central (2008). *China Gateway*. Web site: http://www.biomedcentral.com/gateways/china

China issues trial standards for online education. (2001, June 21). *People's Daily Online*. Retrieved March 20, 2008, from http://english.peopledaily.com.cn/200106/21/eng20010621_73116.html.

Conghui Fang, Xiaochun Zhu. (2006). The open access movement in China. Interlending & Document Supply, 34(4), 186-193. Retrieved April 2, 2008, from ABI/INFORM Global database. (Document ID: 1164893991).

Desktop battle looms in China, Red Flag VP says (2005, December). eWEEK.com Retrieved April 7, 2008, from http://www.destoplinux.com/news/NS7831716922.html

How the open source movement has changed education: 10 success stories. (2007, March 1) OnlineEducation Database website. Retrieved March 25, 2008, from http://oedb.org/library/features/how-the-open-source-movement-has-changed-education-10-success-stories

IOC warns China over web access. (2008, April 1).BBC. Retrieved April 5, 2008, from http://news.bbc.co.uk/2/hi/asia-pacific/7324155.stm.

Liu, B. (2002, November 5). China to be a stronghold for open source. *Internetnews.com*. Retrieved March 18, 2008, from http://www.internetnews.com/dev-news/article.php/1494881

Marson, I. (2005, November 14). China: Local software for local people. *CNET Networks Inc.* Retrieved April 3, 2008, from http://news.com.com/China+Local+software+for+local+people/2100-7344_3-5951629.html

Online and adult education. (2006). *China.org.cn*. Retrieved March 25, 2008, from http://www.china.org.cn/english/features/Brief/192127.htm

Bekkers, T. (n.d.). Open educational resources (OERs): Introduction booklet and webinar. The OER dgCommunity of The Development Gateway Foundation. Retrieved March 10, 2008, from http://openeducation.developmentgateway.org/uploads/media/oer_public/OER_Introduction_Booklet.pdf

Pan, G. & Bonk, C. (2007). The emergence of open-source software in China. *International Review of Research in Open and Distance Learning*, 8 (1). Retrieved April 15, 2008, from http://www.irrodl.org.proxy2.library.uiuc.edu/index.php/irrodl/article/view/331/777

Suber, P. (2002, September 3). China has blocked access to Google. Message posted to Open Access News. Retrieved March 27, 2008, from http://www.earlham.edu/~peters/fos/2002/09/china-has-blocked-access-to-google.html

Wang, T. and Crook, C.K. (2006). The Experiment of Tertiary Online Education in China: An Overview. International. *Journal of Instructional Technology and Distance Learning*, 3(9). Retrieved March 20, 2008, from http://itdl.org/Journal/Sep_06/article01.htm

What should China do? (2005, December 26). *China Daily*. Retrieved March 21, 2008, form http://www.chinadaily.com.cn/english/doc/2005-12/26/content_506502.htm

Yang, Chen Nan (2007, April 27). *China's open source software contest winners announced*. Retrieved April 03, 2008, from Linux.com Web site: http://www.linux.com/articles/61610

Yeates, S. (2005, August 19). Open source in China. EDUCAUSE Connect. Message posted to http://connect.educause.edu/blog/StuartYeates/opensourceandchina/1046?time=1209464038

Lucinda Morgan
University of Illinois at Urbana-Champaign

PEDAGOGY AND LEARNING

FAITH MCKINNEY

9. OPEN EDUCATIONAL RESOURCES FOR K-12 TEACHERS

INTRODUCTION

The Review of the Open Education Resources (OER) Movement: Achievements, Challenges, and New Opportunities – February 2007 for Hewlett Foundation is mainly focusing on the resources that are available for universities and colleges in the United States and around the world. This plan is to be a strategic international development initiative for education. It is to set a precedence of activities culminating in free access to high-quality content to be used by colleges and individuals in the United States and throughout the world to increase human capital. The impact on the developing world is still modest compared to the need ($12 million to non-US institutes). The Hewlett Foundation estimates that of the total $68 million that has been spent, $43 million has gone to the creation and dissemination of the open source content. $25 million has gone into reducing technological barriers, creating understanding of open source content and the stimulation of open source content use. (Atkins, 2007) This a very noble effort and the report talks about the various projects that have been started through this foundation. I would like to look in depth at this report on the various open source content that is available for K-12 teachers. Many students are able to learn concepts and ideas much quicker through the use of games or other teaching methods available on the internet. This need not intimidate teachers. Teachers are still needed to guide the students through their studies. We as educators need to look at a different way of teaching content. In the pages that follow I will look at the challenges and roadblocks that this type of teaching and learning may cause and look at the future of these resources and how we can continue to build and, improve them while getting the word out.

HIGHLIGHTS AND EXAMPLES

The first example I would like to look at is supported by the Hewlett Foundation and dozens of collaborations with OER Partners and communities across the globe. I feel this is one of the most extensive and thorough resources for K-12 learning resources available on the internet today - Open Educational Resources (OER) Commons. OER Commons was created and produced by ISKME, the Institute for the Study of Knowledge Management in Education. The Hewlett Foundation started a great resource for K-12 teachers and I would like to see more done for these K-12 teachers. ISKME is an independent, non-profit educational think tank

M.A. Peters and R.G. Britez (eds.), Open Education and Education for Openness, 107–113.

whose mission is to understand and improve how schools, colleges, universities, and the organizations and agencies that supports them, build their capacity to systematically collect and share information. In addition they apply to well-defined problems and create knowledge-driven environments focused on learning and success. This learning and success is through the use of assessment data to improve classroom instruction; the use of professional development to catalyze change; the use of evaluative findings to improve programs and policy; the use of research to engage practice; or the use of open education content to advance learning opportunities for all learners." (OER Commons, 2007) OER Commons is a global teaching and learning network of free-to-use resources from K-12 lesson plans to college courseware for teachers to use, tag, rate, and review. "OER Commons is the first comprehensive open learning network where teachers and professors (from pre-K to graduate school) can access their colleagues' course materials, share their own, and collaborate on affecting today's classrooms. It uses Web 2.0 features (tags, ratings, comments, reviews, and social networking) to create an online experience that engages educators in sharing their best teaching and learning practices" (OER Commons, 2007).

OER Commons is divided into grade levels, primary (K-8), secondary (9-12) and post-secondary (13+). This chapter will be concentrating on the K-12 portion. In an initial search, there are over 4,500 resources for the primary level and over 6,000 resources for the secondary level. These resources can be filtered in a variety of ways such as:

- Subject Areas of Resource – Arts, Business, Humanities, Math, Statistics, Science, Social Science
- Language of Resource – English, Estonian, French, German, Greek, Italian, Japanese, Polish, Russian, or Spanish. (Most of the resources are in English)
- Course Related Materials – Full Course or Learning Modules (most resources are learning modules)
- Course Related Components – Activities and Labs, Assessments, Audio Lectures, Games, Lecture Notes, Lesson Plans, Syllabi, Textbooks and Readings, Training Material and Video Lectures
- Media Formats – Audio, Video, Graphics/Photos, Downloadable docs, etc.

I looked in detail at the games on this site. Most of the games are hosted or housed on Qedoc Quiz Player. Qedoc is a desktop application for playing quizzes created with the Qedoc Quiz Maker. The desktop application is available as freeware (no cost) to anyone. The main philosophy behind the software is to bring a greater degree of interactivity (and therefore pedagogical depth) to computer-based learning technologies, and to combine this with a greater degree of fun and motivation (Qedoc Quiz Player, 2007). After much time of working through this website, there is a great wealth of resources for teachers. Even the looking up of resources can take valuable time that teachers today do not have. Here are a few suggestions and tips.

- When clicking on a game resource that used Qedoc, simply click on the link at the right side of the page under, "put it on a web page" and the link will take you directly to the game.

- Many of the sources will show detailed lesson plans with activities included to reinforce the concept.
- When needing supplemental material or if wanting to use another resource, use as many details as possible to get the correct topic and games available.
- Many of the sites will ask for an individual to sign in, don't let this discourage you, this is usually free and just a way for the sources to keep track of who uses them.

Another resource highlighted in the Review of the OER Movement is Carnegie Mellon Open Learning Institute (OLI). "OLI grew out of collaboration among cognitive scientists, experts in human computer interaction and seasoned faculty who have both a deep expertise in their respective fields and a strong commitment to excellence in higher education" (Smith, 2008). The majority of the funding for this project is from the Hewlett Foundation but there are other sources as well. For the courses related to Causal and Statistical Reasoning, there were three different additional sources: A.W. Mellon Foundation, James S. McDonnell Foundation and the Fund for the Improvement of Post-Secondary Education. Additional funding for the development of the virtual chemistry lab was supported by the National Science Foundation through the Course, Curriculum and Laboratory Improvement program and the National Science Digital Library. Additional funding for the logic course has received support from the Buhl Foundation and the National Science Foundation, as well as from the Department of Philosophy and Carnegie Mellon. Currently, the project is supported by National Science Foundation grant 0618806 (Mathematical Science Division, CCLI – Expansion Projects) and Carnegie Mellon Qatar. Support for the Andes Physics tutor was developed at the University of Pittsburgh and the United States Naval Academy with support from the Cognitive Science Program of the Office of Naval Research. And finally in the statistics course, StattTtor is based upon work supported by the National Science Foundation and the PEW Foundation. This continues to show that one funding source never seems to be enough and the need for continued support to online teaching resources is needed but also needs to be disseminated to all teachers (Smith, 2008).

OLI courses include a number of innovative online instructional components such as, cognitive tutors, virtual laboratories, group experiments and simulations. At first glance these may not seem like K-12 resources but, they can be used in the secondary classroom in various ways. At the moment this site has courses in the following subject areas, biology, chemistry, physics, casual reasoning, logics and proofs, economics, statistics, engineering statics and French. These are complete courses that teachers can use but I think the best use is as a supplement to teaching. Many topics could be taught and demonstrated in the classroom or they can be used to re-teach a concept that a student did not grasp during a lesson. Many times there can be a personality conflict between teacher and student and the student has either blocked out the teaching methods of the teacher or cannot get past the personality conflict. This is another way for a student to learn the same information from another source and still be able to succeed in the course (Smith, 2008).

Another resource that I would like to look at is HippoCampus. HippoCampus is a project of the Monterey Institute for Technology and Education (MITE). The goal of HippoCampus is to provide high-quality, multimedia content on general education subjects to high school and college students free of charge. HippoCampus was designed as part of Open Education Resources (OER), a worldwide effort to improve access to quality education for everyone. HippoCampus content has been developed by some of the finest colleges and universities in the world and contributed to the National Repository of Online Courses (NROC), another MITE project. The NROC is a growing library of high-quality online courses for students and faculty in higher education, high school and Advanced Placement. NROC makes editorial and engineering investment in the content to prepare it for distribution by HippoCampus. Both HippoCampus and NROC are supported by The William and Flora Hewlett Foundation" (Cook, 2008).

HippoCampus is a full and complete site of courses and can be a great tool for high school teachers. This can be used in class to teach a concept or various parts of the lessons could be used for supplemental teaching as well. There are audio lessons that students can listen to and watch to understand some portions of a subject. The subjects are limited on this website and include: Algebra, American Government, Biology, Calculus, Environmental Science, Physics, Psychology, Religion and US History (Cook, 2008). There are many classes for each area and most of them have audio lessons with them as well. All of these subjects are in English, except for Calculus which is also offered in Spanish. I like this concept and hope there will be more subject lessons in different languages in the future. At the moment these are very limited.

There are a vast amount of resources available on the internet and these are some of the areas that are supported by the Hewlett Foundation. It is vital that all teachers are aware of these projects and resources and it is important for teachers to be updated on the new sources that are continuing to make progress on the internet.

CHALLENGES AND ROADBLOCKS

When talking with educators, there will always be challenges and roadblocks for these internet resources to become a reality in the classroom. One of the main challenges is to have the equipment and the technology available to all teachers in all schools. Another challenge or roadblock is the fear or lack of knowledge of how to use the internet effectively in the classroom. Finally, this resource needs to be embraced by principals, superintendents, and finally our government to understand the need of these resources not only for classroom teachers but also for the students.

We all know that equipment, such as computers and internet connections are a reality today in most homes but many of the schools are lacking. A study in 1999 by the National Center of Educational Statistics reported that 99 percent of all public school teachers had some sort of access to computers and the internet in their schools. Out of this 99 percent of teachers only 34-39 percent of these teachers used it for creating instructional material and or administrative record keeping (NCES, 2008).

Michigan's Freedom to Learn (FTL) initiative, an effort to provide middle school students and teachers with access to wireless laptop computers, has been credited with improving grades, motivation and discipline in classrooms across the state, with one exemplary school seeing reading proficiency scores on the Michigan Education Assessment Program (MEAP) test, administered in January 2005, reportedly increasing from 29 percent to 41 percent for seventh graders and from 31 percent to 63 percent for eighth graders (eSchool News, 2005) (Honey, 2005).

According to the NEA Survey of Educational Technologies in US Schools, "almost all public school educators had access to a computer and to the Internet somewhere in their schools, and the majority had access to computers in their classrooms or primary work areas as well. However, most educators had access to just one or two computers in their classrooms, and only a few had more than five classroom computers for their students' use." (NEA, 2004) The report goes on to say that there is one computer for every five students in public schools nationwide. This number is very deceptive. "The reported ratio is computed by "dividing the total number of students in all public schools by the total number of instructional computers with Internet access in all public schools (i.e., including schools with no Internet access)." (NCES 2002) A survey done in all states showed that the more accurate ratio of computers to students is 10 to 15 students to one computer. This report is even more telling than some of the statistics actually show. The following conclusions were made:

- Students Lack Adequate Access to Computers in the Classroom
- Technical Support is Inadequate
- Educators Want More and Better Training in Using Technology for Instruction
- Technology is Not Sufficiently Used for Instruction
- Technology Gaps Remain for Particular Groups of Schools, Teachers, and Students
- Educators' Perceptions of Technology Are Significantly Associated with their Job Experiences (NEA, 2004)

One talks of all the different resources available online and the open educational resources and yet if the technology is not available in United States where many of these resources are developed, how can we expect them to be accessed from other countries who have less technology access than the United States?

LOOKING TOWARD THE FUTURE

Technology has continue to advance in our world and we as educators need to make sure that our teaching styles and student learning stays up with this continued advancement. As noted before from the NEA survey, financial issues usually play the major role in this issue. In looking toward the future, I'd like to address the key conclusions from the NEA Report.

Computers and the Internet need to be made available in all classrooms or primary work areas at a ratio that allows students to gain regular and unencumbered access throughout the school day (NEA, 2004). This is something that each state needs to make a priority. We talk about educating our students to be able to function in the world and without this tool many students will be "left behind". One possibility is to use the money that is spent on textbooks and divert it. Textbooks are usually outdated before they are printed and moving away from the textbook and working directly with objectives might be a move in the right direction.

A more integrated and broad-scale approach to providing equipment upgrades and technical support should be devised through staff training and district planning (NEA, 2004). This needs to be a priority of states and districts. Computers can be put in all schools but they must be supported and maintained so that if something goes wrong they can be repaired.

Training on using technology has not been adequate to prepare most educators to use technology for instruction. Instructional staff in public schools uses technology primarily for applications such as word processing rather than direct instruction of students, and the degree of use in instruction varies widely between demographic groups (NEA, 2004). As an educator of twenty plus years, I did not go through school when computers were a common learning tool. There are many educators in this same situation and those that are older may have resistance to this new method of teaching. Teachers who are willing to use technology may feel they haven't been taught how to use these new tools adequately. Again school districts need to take a serious role and make technology training a mandatory professional development piece for all teachers.

Substantial gaps in technology access are still evident for particular demographic and geographic groups, such as between high- and low-poverty schools; early, mid-, and late career professionals; elementary, middle, and high schools; and in different regions of the country (NEA, 2004). This is an issue that will continue to be discussed but state education departments and school districts need to provide an education to all students regardless of economic status. Resources must be made available to all schools and all students.

Until this is made a priority from the federal level on down, many students in our schools will never have the access necessary for them to succeed in our world and in their future.

BIBLIOGRAPHY

Cook, Nancy (2008) *About HippoCampus*. Retrieved April 7, 2008 from http://hippocampus.org/jsp/about.jsp?&from=/

Honey, Margaret, & Spielvogel, Robert (2005) *Critical Issue: Using Technology to Improve Student Achievement*. Retrieved April, 7, 2008, from http://www.ncrel.org/sdrs/areas/issues/methods/technlgy/te800.htm#context.

National Center of Educational Statistics. (2000) *Stats Brief: Teacher Use of Computers and the Internet in Public Schools*. Jessup, MD: Author

National Education Association. (2004) *Gains and Gaps in Education Technology*. Washington, D.C.: Author.

Open Educational Resources Commons (2007). *Linking you to Teaching and Learning Resources.* Retrieved April 7, 2008 from http://www.oercommons.org/

Qedoc Quiz Player (2007). Retrieved April 7, 2008 from http://www.qedoc.org/en/index.php?title=Qedoc_ Quiz_Player Smith, Joel, & Thille, Candace (2008) *Innovative Components.* Retrieved April 7, 2008 from http://www.cmu.edu/oli/overview/index.html.
The William and Flora Hewlett Foundation. (2007) A Review of the Open Educational Resources (OER) Movement: Achievements, Challenges, and New Opportunities. San Francisco. Atkins, D.E., Brown, J.S., Hammond, A.L.

Faith McKinney
Program Developer
International Programs, Asia
California State University, Fullerton

LINDA SMITH TABB

10. APPLYING AN OPEN EDUCATION ECOSYSTEM TO FOREIGN LANGUAGE TEACHING AND LEARNING

INTRODUCTION

The teaching of languages in the American context is accompanied by issues of terminology that are in flux. Language teaching and the choices made concerning which languages should be learned have long been political, but the terms used to describe those languages are now in the process of shifting. The traditional term *foreign languages* seems to still hold favor in the U.S., noting that despite the widespread use of *world languages* by many, the American Council for the Teaching of Foreign Languages (ACTFL) has not yet changed its name. By establishing an Ad Hoc Committee on Foreign Languages, the Modern Languages Association (MLA) has reinforced the traditional terminology.

Also in flux are the models of language instruction at all levels including higher education, as well as a policy shift at the national level in the hierarchy of importance in the study of certain languages termed 'critical need foreign languages' by the Bush administration. While the MLA is calling for more study of history, culture, economics and society in the context of language study, in the backdrop is the National Security Language Initiative (NSLI), a policy to further strengthen national security and prosperity in the 21st century through education, especially in developing foreign language skills. The NSLI was created at the beginning of 2006 to dramatically increase the number of Americans learning so-called critical need foreign languages such as Arabic, Chinese, Russian, Hindi, Farsi, and others, through new and expanded programs from kindergarten through university and into the workforce. A white paper by the U.S. Defense Department entitled 'Call to Action for National Foreign Language Capabilities' outlines the importance given to foreign language learning as a goal in the context of national security in the post 9/11 world. All the while, some common languages of study in the U.S., such as German, are seeing whole departments eliminated at places like the University of Southern California (USC), even despite healthy enrollments (Jaschik, 2008).

This would be complicated enough if foreign language teaching and learning were prioritized in American schools and institutions of higher learning, but they quite often are not. Policies such as No Child Left Behind (NCLB) and issues of money and allocation of scarce resources make the teaching and learning of languages in K-12 a low priority in many schools. Unlike other academic

M.A. Peters and R.G. Britez (eds.), Open Education and Education for Openness, 115–125.

disciplines, language learning is skill-based, and beginning skills are taught at the beginning, regardless of the age and level of instruction. So later access to language learning in elementary and secondary schools impacts ultimate mastery of foreign languages in higher education institutions, as well as the accomplishment of the more lofty, but useful goal of *multilingualism* (mother tongue + 2) now prevalent in the European Union.

ADDRESSING THE U.S. LANGUAGE DEFICIT: FROM OPEN SPACE TO OPEN SOURCE

It was my involvement as a participant in something called 'Open Space Technology' at *ConnectEd, A Conference on Global Education* held at the Monterey Conference Center in Monterey, California in January, 2008 that helped me to focus my thinking and ideas about issues concerning foreign language education in the U.S. I was able to connect the Open Space environment and collaboration of participants in discussion, with the Open Source ideas that I had been reading about and discussing in a course taught at the University of Illinois by Michael Peters entitled, "Open Access, Open Source, Open Education".

According to Lisa Heft,

> Open Space is a method used around the world for convening participant-driven conferences, retreats and work meetings. Open Space is used to convene people for participatory decision-making, interdisciplinary task work and understanding each other across differences.

Open Space is not unlike Open Source in that it is a tool that can cut across boundaries and enable people to accomplish work together in new and different ways. Discussion groups are created through a process that involves an opening circle and an agenda wall. After starting and facilitating a group of my own, I made my way to a new group discussion entitled, "How do we address the U.S. language deficit?" started by Clara Yu and Amy McGill. It was a lively discussion that touched on many issues I had long contemplated throughout my professional career having taught not one, but two different foreign languages in the U.S. Because of my experience teaching at the middle school, high school, community college and university levels, much of the discussion was familiar to me. Foreign language professionals seem to have these same discussions everywhere, and it was not hard for many of us to find our thoughts and ideas echoed in each others' voices.

But then, something happened. The discussion went in a new direction. It was suggested that if what is happening now in the schools and institutions in the U.S. isn't working, then something new needs to happen, something outside of our traditional learning institutions. This new thing should work from the bottom up, and be attractive to every student, and therefore be learner-centered. Why should students want to learn a language for someone else's purposes? Since money is the issue so often used as an excuse to not add foreign language offerings and programs, this new thing must be inexpensive. Online and Open Source Foreign

Language Learning was mentioned as a possibility that fulfils all of these requirements.

Open educational resources are being created all over the world and allow learners to connect across boundaries, and across languages. Creation and experimentation in this area abound, giving the learner new freedoms – freedom to choose the language and level appropriate to his or her needs, and freedom to learn at a pace of one's own choosing.

OPEN EDUCATION PUTS LEARNERS AND LEARNING AT THE CENTER

Carl Rogers considered learning as a freedom. Rogers himself stated in his book, *Freedom to Learn*, that a way must be found to develop a climate in the system in which the focus is not upon teaching, but on the facilitation of self-directed learning. Rogers saw "self-directed learning" as the ultimate goal of education (Tabb, 2005). One of the futures of the student-centered approach may well be in online foreign language learning and open education, and with the use of new technologies that facilitate this approach, drawing learners who are open to innovative new approaches and self-directed learning.

Self-directed learning is the hallmark of Autonomous Technology Assisted Language Learning (ATALL). ATALL refers to the development and use of technological tools to facilitate foreign language learning, and the research on the use of such tools.

> ATALL provides a means for language learners to improve their L2 proficiency whether or not they are taking formal courses in the language they are learning. ATALL can be used by students in conjunction with formal L2 study or by learners who are not taking L2 classes. ATALL is based on the latest theory and research on Second Language Acquisition (SLA), the psychology of learning and Computer Assisted Language Learning (CALL), and principles of this theory and research are applied to the development of ATALL tools and activities (Cziko, 2007).

The term L1 is used to refer to the first or native language, and the term L2 can refer to any language learned after learning the L1, regardless of whether it is the first, second, third, fourth or even fifth language (Mitchell, 2004; Gass, 2007).

AN OPEN EDUCATION ECOSYSTEM

At the 2007 iSummit in Dubrovnik, Croatia there was a full track dedicated to open education. The iSummit is organized annually by iCommons and is a gathering of people from the global Creative Commons movement. One of the things they did in the open education track was to develop a series of five drawings to show what the future of open education might look like (Schmidt & Surman, 2007). Together the five drawings create a sketch of what is being called an 'open education ecosystem' with learning in the center, and people, organizations, communities, content and tools surrounding it and interacting with it. In addition, values and processes also impact the learning with such actions as advocacy, accreditation, alliance building, creating, improving, using, teaching, remixing, peer production, policy making, community building, localizing, packaging, marketing and licensing all playing a role in the ecosystem (Schmidt & Surman, 2007). These processes show how vital and alive the community is that resides in the non-living environment of the ecosystem itself.

In order to understand more clearly how open access, open source and open education are functioning, it is best to look at not just their component parts, but to look at how the component parts form a system. The following were identified at iSummit 2007 as the component parts:

- People ~ Open education space is populated by students, authors, educators, self-directed learners, policy makers and administrators. Often individuals will play more than one role.
- Communities ~ Peer production communities and writing teams create content. Communities of practice share information and knowledge between members working in similar areas, and include policy networks and localization clubs. There has been little effort made to more formally build these two communities.
- Organizations ~ Diploma and degree and credential granting institutions such as schools and universities, governments, INGOs, businesses, funders, and informal learning groups
- Tools ~ These are the things used to engage in open education, including content searches, repositories, writing platforms, but also the various forms of licenses.

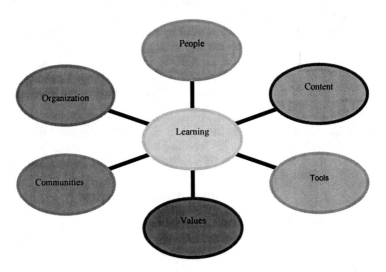

Figure 1: Diagram of an open education ecosystem

Note: This diagram is adapted from "Open sourcing education: Learning and wisdom from iSummit 2007" by J.P. Schmidt and M. Surman, September 2, 2007.

– Values ~ Common values shared globally hold the ecosystem together. Key words such as 'user centered', 'open', 'collaborative', 'globally connected', locally driven' describe the common ground for the system.

– Content ~ Includes textbooks, teaching notes, online courseware, educational software, games, etoys, learning designs, learner created content and peer to peer learning applications.

– Processes are the actions the people take within the system, and are not shown on the diagram. It is best to imagine them moving into, around and through the component parts in an ongoing swirl of constant motion, changing each component in their paths, as well as connecting the components in a multitude of ways. It is the creative force of these actions that make the system dynamic and living.

This model helps to broaden the scope of our understanding of open education, but even so, there is still an emphasis on content and tools, rather than on use and learning. According to Schmidt and Surman (2007), "processes, communities, institutions and, most importantly, people are all central to making open education a success."

APPLYING THE OPEN EDUCATION ECOSYSTEM MODEL TO FOREIGN LANGUAGE LEARNING

I found the ecosystem model to be helpful in mapping out the open education movement as it applies to foreign language learning. It became clear during my research that there were more tools and content items than anything else, but although many of the articles and blogs discussed content and tools, others also discussed organizations, communities and people. This model helped make sense of the role of each, and the interrelationship between and among the constituent parts. I will use the same categories to describe an example of an open education ecosystem in area of foreign language learning.

– People ~ The people involved in language learning in open education cross borders and are not limited to one geographical area of the world. This is one major difference in open education. Authors, teachers, learners and policy makers can be located in different places and still be able to be involved. Native speakers need not leave a place where the language is spoken to teach others who are wanting to learn a new language. Learners are not limited by the policy makers in their own area whose policy might preclude them from learning a certain language at a particular stage of life. Everything about language learning, teaching and policy making is opened up to a new landscape and new opportunities. In addition, people can work together across differences of time and space as well as age, gender, disability, race, culture, religion and many other barriers that might serve to separate in other more conventional environments.

– Communities ~ Some examples of communities include the OJS community, Curriki Groups, and OpenLearn Learning Space discussion forum boards. OJS is a multilingual system, allowing journals to publish in a variety of languages and is a part of PKP, the Public Knowledge Project. OJS currently publishes in fifteen languages and is currently in the process of adding eight more. Curriki: The Global Education and Learning Community has established Curriki Groups. Curriki members can form a group around any subject area, grade level, or educational philosophy. This is where members meet, share ideas, and work collaboratively with other educators. The OpenLearn website gives free access to course materials from The Open University. The LearningSpace is open to learners anywhere in the world, and has a Modern Languages forum to encourage community interaction. Communities such as 'Webheads in Action' create content.

–   Organizations ~ Several different types of organizations are involved in open education involving foreign languages. On the local level, these include schools and institutions of learning of all kinds. These also include international organizations like UNESCO and OECD, and the Open Society Institute. They also include foundations such as the Free Software Foundation, the Linux Foundation, the Mozilla Foundation, the Apache Software Foundation, the Development Gateway Foundation, and the William and Flora Hewlett Foundation. Several universities have played a key role. These include pioneers such as the Open University in UK, MIT, Rice, Carnegie Mellon, and Stanford, who have led the way for an ongoing involvement by these types of institutions. Also some businesses such as Apple, Microsoft and Sun Microsystems are becoming involved. Because national governments and government entities such as the U.S. Department of Defense are organizations that create foreign language policy, they play a role. In addition, governments and their entities can choose to allow or censor content online, as well as set up surveillance scenarios which impact the availability and perceived desirability of open education. Some supranational organizations such as the European Union have also made language policy which impacts individual learners as well as content creation for open education entities such as the Open University.

–   Tools ~ One commonly used tool is a content repository. Many of the organizations and universities that are most involved in open education have established content repositories affiliated with them. These include Rice's Connexions, Carnegie Mellon's Open Learning Initiative, and Open University's OpenLearn Learning Space. Other content repositories include OER Commons Open Educational Resources, dgCommunities, and MERLOT World Languages Portal. Repositories are considered tools because they are used to make it easier to find and share content. Tools such as search engines like Google can be used as informative tools, collaborative tools, communicative tools, and as aggregative tools in language learning (Chinnery, 2008). Other tools such as open source online platforms like Moodle enable instruction in multiple languages. This semester I taught a French course at the University of Illinois using a Moodle course site that was in French. Wikis made in PBwiki and blogs in WordPress are also easily adapted as tools for language learning, especially at higher levels where writing is emphasized. TiddlyWiki is a personal wiki that allows the storage of text fragments in a non-linear manner, allowing you to tag each tiddler creating an useful language wiki (Popov, 2006). Applications such as RSS feed readers, Technorati, del.icio.us and Google Docs have wide application in language learning and in other disciplines. Other tools lend themselves quite handily to the needs of the foreign language teacher and learner. Quick Key 5.2 is an open source keyboard extension that allows the typing of all 65,000 characters that exist today. Audacity is a free, easy-to-use audio editor and recorder for Windows, Mac OS X, GNU/Linux, and other operating systems that can be used to record words and expressions and make language podcasts or record a radio program (Popov, 2006).These recordings can then be hosted at Odeo. New combinations in the use of cell phones and web applications are beginning to be seen as well. jVLT is a vocabulary learning tool which can be used for foreign languages. jMemorize is a free open-source Java application that manages learning processes by using flashcards and can easily be used for foreign language vocabulary. StarDict is a cross-platform and international dictionary software. Find out how to say a word at Forvo, which includes the pronunciation of words in twenty-three languages. English learners can work on vocabulary using Learnit. And of course innovative teachers and learners can use many of the common open source applications for a multitude of uses. Pictures of vocabulary words can be shared using Flickr, and slide shows of grammar explanations can be posted and shared using SlideShare. Videos can be made and shared using YouTube and downloaded using ClipNabber. Need to create a cartoon and use authentic writing in the speech bubbles? Try ToonDooo. Want to create a game? Use ClassTools.net. Want to keep practicing your language with another speaker? Use Vawkr. Skype, an Internet telephone company enables nine users to conference-call on its free service facilitating the interaction of groups of learners across both boundaries and languages. Computer games such as massively multiplayer online role-playing games (MMORPGs) and virtual worlds, such as Second Life show great promise as innovations in online language learning pedagogy. For an open source presentation on this topic, see http://www.slideshare.net/bcgstanley/wiaoc2007-games-may-2007 Computer-assisted language learning (CALL) is changing very quickly with three major trends that are significant. These include convergence, innovations in searchability, and collaboration (Hanson-Smith, 2008). Each of these three trends are reflected in the tools that are available to people with open access, using open education through the use of open source tools. These trends and their alignment with the values of the ecosystem of open education have huge potential to change the landscape of language learning not just in the U.S., but globally.

– Values ~ The values associated with the open education movement are widely applicable to the teaching and learning of foreign language. Openness is an important part of learning a language. Since language learning is based on skill-building, a user-centered approach is important. Since language is by its very nature social, being globally connected offers more advantages than ever before for interacting with speakers of the target language and for collaboration across time, space and boundaries. Open education creates a new social context in which language learning can take place. Since the social context in which language learning occurs leads to attitudes on the part of learners, an interactive, collaborative environment with access to target language speakers online can impact the motivation of learners (Mitchell & Myles, 2004).

— Content ~ "Traditionally, most of the energy and money in open education have gone into producing content, and most of it in developed countries" (Schmidt & Shurman, 2007). Many people think mostly of content when they consider the open education movement, not recognizing the interplay of all of the other parts of the ecosystem. Content in the discipline of foreign language learning is high in variety. On MERLOT alone, there are 1,955 separate listings of web-based content in world languages. These consist of online texts and teaching notes, educational software products, language learning games and learner created content. Open courseware from universities includes language units, modules and whole courses. Lingro is a new language learning website. Working with the open source philosophy, lingro has created dictionaries for learners of English, Spanish, French, German, Italian and Polish. These dictionaries are open source. The content-rich site also has linked together the means to create a wordlist and has both a web viewer and a file viewer to facilitate vocabulary learning (Gallen, 2008). Mango languages is another new site that has free language lessons with interactive slides with a range of languages including English, Spanish, French, German, Greek, Italian, Japanese, Portuguese, and Mandarin, and a way to work between the different languages, for example from Spanish to English. Live Mocha is an e-learning start up which offers the collaborative advantages of Web 2.0 social networking. "Writingmatrix is an extensive online project that involves key elements essential to collaboration in Web 2.0, such as aggregation, tagging and social networking" (Stevens, Quintana, Zeinstejer, Sirk, Molero, & Arena, 2008). The innovation in both the tools and content of the open education ecosystem as applied to foreign language continues to grow and change rapidly.

— Processes ~ All of the actions normally associated with the open education ecosystem apply broadly to foreign language learning and teaching. Communities are built. Content is localized and peer produced. Policies are made. Programs are accredited. Alliances are built. Teaching of certain languages is advocated. Content packages are licensed, packaged and marketed. Languages are taught. Tools and content are created, improved, used and remixed. The foreign language open education ecosystem is a vital and living thing, and it is an open system in constant motion.

THE DISCONNECT BETWEEN POLICY AND PRACTICE: CLOSED SYSTEMS AND OPEN SYSTEMS

In conclusion, foreign language policies are often set both locally and nationally, by school boards, university administrations, state governments and national governments. These policies seek to direct the learning of languages from above in the context of schools and universities, in a closed system that has as an assumption the closing down of boundaries and borders.

In contrast, while the U.S. National Security Language Initiative, an extreme example of a closed national policy was being sketched out, an entire other world was opening up. This online world of language learning through open access, open source and open education is a dynamic open system with no borders or boundaries, and is a push from below. The online environment blurs the differentiation between foreign language learning and second language acquisition creating the possibility of a new type of environment, space and social context which is more difficult to quantify, and where new opportunities exist.

Foreign Language learning generally is differentiated from second language acquisition in that the former refers to the learning of a nonnative language in the environment of one's native language. Second language acquisition, on the other hand, generally refers to the learning of nonnative language in the environment in which that language is spoken (Gass & Selinker, 2007, p. 7).

There is a clear disconnect between policy and practice, and closed and open systems in foreign language teaching and learning in today's changing world. While government entities are encouraging the learning of certain languages for the good not of the learner, but of the state, learners are free to choose to study languages outside the context of traditional classrooms in a borderless open world of self-directed learning online. They can do this any time day or night, and anywhere they have open access to the Internet. By doing so, they become a part of the growing foreign language open education ecosystem that is changing as I type these words.

REFERENCES

Abbey, K. (2007). Review of Google docs. *Currents in Electronic Literacy*. Retrieved April 26, 2008, from http://currents.cwrl.utexas.edu/spring07/abbey

Arena, C. (2008). Blogging in the language classroom: It doesn't "simply happen". *TESL-EJ: Teaching English as Second or Foreign Language*, *11*(4), 1–7. Retrieved April 26, 2008, from http://tesl-ej.org/ej44/toc.html

Blackall, L. (2008). Open educational resources and practices. *TESL-EJ: Teaching English as Second or Foreign Language*, *11*(4), 1–19. Retrieved April 26, 2008, from http://tesl-ej.org/ej44/toc.html

Blankenship, L. (2007). *Podcasting in education: A perspective from Bryn Mawr college*. Retrieved April 26, 2008, from http://www.academiccommons.org/commons/essay/blankenship-podcasting

Bryant, T. (2006). *Using World of Warcraft and other MMORPGs to foster a targeted, social, and cooperative approach to language learning*. Retrieved on April 26, 2008, from http://www.academiccommons/essay/bryant-MMORPGs-for-SLA

Bump, J. (2007). Teaching English in second life. *Currents in Electronic Literacy*. Retrieved April 26, 2008, from http://currents.cwrl.utexas.edu/spring07/bump

Chinnery, G. M. (2008). You've got some GALL: Google-assisted language learning. *Language Learning &Technology*, *12*, 3–11.

Curriki: The Global Education & Learning Community. Retrieved January 24, 2008, from http://www.curriki.org/xwiki/bin/view/Main/WebHome

Cziko, G. (2007). *Autonomous technology-assisted language learning*. Retrieved May 12, 2008, from http://cnx.org/content/m15244/latest

Forvo: All the words in the world pronounced. Retrieved April 21, 2008, from http://www.forvo.com/

LINDA SMITH TABB

Gallen, M. (2008). *Lingro.com: Open source language learning.* Retrieved from April 20, 2008, from http://eduspaces.net/mlgallen/weblog/296630.html

Gass, S. M., & Selinker, L. (2008). *Second language acquisition: An introductory course* (3rd ed.). New York: Routledge.

Hanson-Smith, E. (2008). Trends in digital media 2007. *TESL-EJ: Teaching English as Second or Foreign Language, 11*(4), 1–13. Retrieved April 26, 2008, from http://tesl-ej.org/ej44/toc.html

Heft, L. (2008). *Open space technology session book.* Retrieved May 12, 2008, from http://www.connectedconference.org/pdf/OST%20Session%20Book.pdf

Hurd, S., & Xiao, J. (2006). Open and distance language learning at the Shantou Radio and TV University, China, and the Open University, United Kingdom: A cross-cultural perspective. *Open Learning, 21*, 205–219.

Learnitlists. Retrieved April 21, 2008, from http://www.learnitlists.com/how-it-works/

Livemocha. Retrieved April 20, 2008, from http://www.livemocha.com/pages/about

Jaschik, S. (2007, January 2). *Dramatic plan for language programs.* Retrieved April 11, 2008, from http://www.insidehighered.com/layout/set/print/news/2007/la

Jaschik, S. (2007, May 24). *Broader vision for languages.* Retrieved April 11, 2008, from http://www.insidehighered.com/layout/set/print/news/2007/05/24/mla

Jaschik, S. (2008, April 11). *Das Ende for German.* Retrieved April 11, 2008, from http://www.insidehighered.com/news/2008/04/11/german

Mango languages. Retrieved April 21, 2008, from http://mashable.com/2007/09/18/trymango/

Merlot world languages portal. Retrieved May 2, 2008, from http://worldlanguages.merlot.org/

Mitchell, R., & Myles, F. (2004). *Second language learning theories* (2nd ed.). New York: Oxford University.

Modern Language Association. (2007). *Foreign languages and higher education: New structures for a changed world.* Retrieved April 11, 2008, from http://www.mla.org/pdf/forlang_news_pdf.pdf

National security language initiative. Retrieved May 12, 2008, from http://www.aau.edu/education/NSLI_FactSheet_3906.pdf

Popov, D. (2006). *Learn foreign languages with open source software.* Retrieved April 21, 2008, from http:// www.linux.com/articles/54605?tid=132&tid=130&tid=138

Public Knowledge Project. *OJS languages.* Retrieved May 2, 2008, from http://pkp.sfu.ca/ojs-languages

Quick key: An open source keyboard extension. Retrieved April 20, 2008, from http://quickkeydotnet.sourceforge.net/

Reciteword. Retrieved April 28, 2008, from http://directory.fsf.org/project/reciteword/

Rogers, C. R. (1969). *Freedom to learn.* Columbus, OH: Merrill.

Ros i Solé, C., & Hopkins, J. (2007). Contrasting two approaches to distance language learning. *Distance Education, 28*, 351–370.

Rundell, M. (2000). The biggest corpus of all. *Humanising Language Teaching, 2*(3). Retrieved May 2, 2008, from http://www.hltmag.co.uk/may00/idea.htm

Schmidt, J. P., & Surman, M. (2007). *Open sourcing education: Learning and wisdom from iSummit 2007.* Retrieved May 12, 2008, from http://learn.ed.uiuc.edu/file.php/385/1189316040_open_sourcing_education_icommon_2007_report_final_1_.pdf

Stanley, G., & Mawer, K. (2008). Language learners & computer games: From space invaders to second life. *TESL-EJ: Teaching English as Second or Foreign Language, 11*(4), 1–12. Retrieved April 26, 2008, from http://tesl-ej.org/ej44/toc.html

Stevens, V., Quintana, N., Zeinstejer, R., Sirk, S., Molero, D., & Arena, C. (2008). Writingmatrix: Connecting students with blogs, tags, and social networking. *TESL-EJ: Teaching English as Second or Foreign Language, 11*(4), 1–16. Retrieved April 26, 2008, from http://tesl-ej.org/ej44/toc.html

Tabb, L. S. (2005). *Classrooms where active listening and student empowerment are essential.* Retrieved May 12, 2008, from http://wik.ed.uiuc.edu/index.php/SKEP_Classrooms_where_active_listening_and_student_empowerment_are_essential

Tremel, J., & Jesson, J. (2007). Podcasting in the rhetoric classroom. *Currents in Electronic Literacy.* Retrieved April 26, 2008, from http://currents.cwrl.utexas.edu/spring07/tremel_and_jesson

124

United Nations Educational, Scientific and Cultural Organization. (2008). *International year of languages*. Retrieved April 21, 2008, from http://portal.unesco.org/culture/en/ev.php-URL_ID=35524&URL

United States Department of Defense. *Call to action for national foreign language capabilities.* Retrieved May 12, 2008, from http://www.nlconference.org/docs/White_Paper.pdf

Zeinstejer, R. (2008). The wiki revolution: A challenge to traditional education. *TESL-EJ: Teaching English as Second or Foreign Language, 11*(4), 1–8. Retrieved April 26, 2008, from http://tesl-ej.org/ej44/toc.html

Linda Smith Tabb
Department of Educational Policy Studies,
University of Illinois at Urbana – Champaign

Department of Humanities
Parkland College

CPSIA information can be obtained
at www.ICGtesting.com
Printed in the USA
FFOW04n1404151015
17728FF

9 789087 906795